MW01005095

DECLASSIFIED
Authority: E.O. 13526
By: NDC NARA Date: Dec 31, 2012

PROJECT ZEBRA

ROOSEVELT AND STALIN'S TOP-SECRET MISSION TO TRAIN 300 SOVIET AIRMEN IN AMERICA

M.G.CRISCI

IN COLLABORATION WITH GREGORY GAGARIN

ORCA PUBLISHING COMPANY USA   2018

Copyright© 2017 by M.G. Crisci

All rights reserved,
Including the right of reproduction
in whole or in part in any form.
Orca Publishing Company, USA

Edited by Robin Friedheim, Holly Scudero
Designed by Good World Media
Photographs and Documents: See References

Library of Congress Case No.
PRE000009623

ISBN-13: 978-1-4566-3252-6 (Amazon KDP)
ISBN-13: 978-1-4566-2864-2 (hardcover)
ISBN-13: 978-1-4566-2863-5 (paperback)

Manufactured in the United States of America

First Edition

Also by M.G. Crisci

7 Days in Russia
Call Sign, White Lily
Donny and Vladdy
Indiscretion
Mary Jackson Peale
Only in New York
Papa Cado
Papa Cado's Book of Wisdom
Project Zebra
Salad Oil King
Save the Last Dance
This Little Piggy

Learn more at

mgcrisci.com
twitter.com/worldofmgcrisci
YouTube.com/worldofmgcrisci
Facebook.com/worldofmgcrisci

Contents

Preface

About seven years ago, I was invited to the Russian Cultural Center in Washington, D.C., to discuss how and why I, an American with no Russian ancestry, came to write a book about the life and times of the world's first female fighter pilot: a Russian teenager named Lilia Litvyak (1921-1943).

At the end of my talk, a tall, distinguished gentleman approached. He introduced himself as Gregory Gagarin and complimented me on my accomplishment, the accuracy of details in *Call Sign, White Lily*, and my ability to collaborate with a broad cross section of Russians and Ukrainians many thousands of miles away. Then: "Would you be interested in another collaboration?"

"About what?" I asked.

"The story of a top-secret World War II mission that's never been told," he said.

Though it sounded intriguing, I declined, citing other projects. Sometime later, I was to speak in Moscow, Russia, about *Call Sign*. Somehow, Gregory heard about my impending trip. He called to ask if I would have dinner with a few of his Russian friends in Moscow. I figured, why not? I met two sisters by the names of Emilia and Yelena Chibisov. They explained their father was a decorated Russian Major General named Maxim Chibisov and that he and "Grigory" had worked together closely during World War II in "North Carolina, America."

Emilia urged me, "Talk to Grigory; he has many of the details."

Upon my return, I visited Grigory's home. He took me on a tour of his extensive collection of historical memorabilia and rather humbly told me that his grandfather was a member of the Imperial Russian Aristocracy. That house tour was my first exposure to the words *Project Zebra*. Four years and hundreds of interviews, documents, and discoveries later, Grigory and I are proud to introduce you to top-secret *Project Zebra:*

"Roosevelt and Stalin's Top-Secret Mission to Train 300 Soviet Airmen in America."

Project Zebra is the only documented instance in history where Soviet flying aces and their crews were trained in America by American Naval officers to fly a huge, American-made amphibious seaplane called the PBN-Nomad. Amazingly, we produced 184 of these state-of-the-art planes in Philadelphia and trained 300+ Soviet airmen in the patriotic town of Elizabeth City, North Carolina, without any media leaks. These heavily armed Nomads went on to seek and destroy numerous Nazi U-boats and Japanese submarines in the Atlantic and Pacific Theaters without losing a single plane.

Top-secret Project Zebra was also a historic human event. The Soviet and American teams shared experiences that created bonds of trust and mutual respect, despite their language barriers and cultural differences — something that might serve us well to model during these uncertain Russian-American moments. Project Zebra was declassified on December 31, 2012, and remains one of WWII's last never-been-told stories. Until now!

The personal stories that comprise the body of this book happened. The vintage photographs and rare military documents are real, as are the stories that have been passed on by word of mouth.

M. G. Crance

Chapter 1

Directive 21

Adolf Hitler and Joseph Stalin celebrate an improbable deal

During World War I, America rallied around President Woodrow Wilson's crusade to "make the world safe for democracy." But time dimmed intent. By the 1930s, critics were convinced US involvement in that war was driven primarily by profit-hungry bankers, war material producers, and arms traders. These widely-held beliefs eventually led the US Senate and House of Representatives to create an isolationist movement via the issuance of a series of Neutrality Acts[1] which, by law, forced America to remain neutral with countries

---

[1] Neutrality Acts of 1935, 37, and 39. Office of the US Historian.

at war. During this same period, Germany and the Soviet Union's aggressive appetites to dominate and control the world grew at an alarming rate.

Differing Dictatorships

Nazism fixated on the racial superiority of the Aryan race, built on a foundation of pseudoscience and biological determinism that placed Jews, blacks, and other minorities in very low regard. Nazism divided human society along strict religious, ethnic, and racial lines.

By contrast, Communism focused on an economic hierarchy known simply as the "haves" and "have-nots." Communism sought to empower the latter (i.e., the have-nots) to revolt against the former.

Despite seeming differences, both Nazism and Communism created and enforced a regimented set of rules for "acceptable" political behavior — painting a very bleak "black-and-white" world with little wiggle room for any divergent political thought.

Nonaggression Pact

On August 23, 1939 — shortly before World War II (1939-45) broke out in Europe — avowed enemies Nazi Germany and the Soviet Union surprised the world by signing the German-Soviet Nonaggression Pact, despite their seemingly different totalitarian world views.

Under the terms of the Nonaggression Pact, Germany and the USSR agreed to take no military action against each other for the next ten years. Stalin viewed the pact as a means of keeping his nation on peaceful terms with Germany while giving him time to build up the Soviet military. Hitler used the pact to make sure Germany could invade Poland unopposed, to expand his geographic base westward and eventually rule the world as the dominant superpower.

Hitler was smart enough — and demonic enough — to realize he couldn't achieve his endgame without the support of what he called the three major Axis Powers — Japan, Italy, and Russia. From various conferences, Hitler knew Japan and Italy, for a variety of reasons, were "all in."

But he was less certain of Stalin's intentions. He knew Stalin believed the success and expansion of America's capitalistic way of life could undermine his brand of communism, but he also knew Stalin had his own interest in world domination.

On September 27, 1940, Germany, Italy, and Japan signed the Axis Pact, which divided the world into spheres of influence and was implicitly directed at the United States. Interestingly, the pact contained a clear provision (Article 5) that the agreement did not include or discuss relations with the Soviet Union.

Hitler-Stalin Rift

During October and November 1940, Germany and the USSR Soviet Axis held unilateral talks concerning the Soviet Union's inclusion as the fourth Axis Power. After the talks, each side provided the other with conflicting written proposed agreements. For example, Hitler encouraged Soviet presence in Iran while removing its influence in the Balkans, and giving Germany full rights to Finland's immense natural resources.

The two parties argued for several weeks. Finally, an impatient Hitler remarked to his top military chiefs that Stalin "demands more and more," "he's a cold-blooded blackmailer," and that "Stalin must be brought to his knees as soon as possible." Hitler decided to leave negotiations unresolved by not responding during the winter and spring of 1941.

London Evening Standard explains the growing Hitler-Stalin rift

Instead, several directives (i.e., top-secret instructions and military plans) were issued directly by Hitler during that period. They covered a wide range of subjects, from detailed direction of World War II military units to the governance of occupied territories and their populations. Under the Nazi system, these directives were binding and followed to the letter, unless superseded by another law.

On the other side of the border, Stalin anticipated an eventual war with Germany, but he badly miscalculated the "when." Speaking to his generals in December 1940, Stalin noted Hitler's references to an inevitable Soviet attack in *Mein Kampf* Publicly, Stalin urged his commanders to always be ready to repulse a German attack.

Privately, he told his tiny inner circle that the Soviet Army would require time to approach equaling the Nazi war machine. "Comrade Commanders, we must do everything in our power to delay the Nazi war for another two years." He also communicated to FDR through his highest-ranking government officials, Foreign Minister Vyacheslav Molotov and Ambassador Maxim Litvinov, that the Nazi Soviet alliance was tactical, the Russians never trusted Hitler, and they were certain he would eventually attempt to invade Russia.

Directive No. 21

During the month of Stalin's reassuring assessment, Hitler asked his commanders to accelerate military plans for a massive invasion of Russia. On December 18, 1940, Hitler signed *Weisung Nr. 21 (Directive No. 21)*, code name Operation Barbarossa. The date for the invasion was set for May 15, 1941.

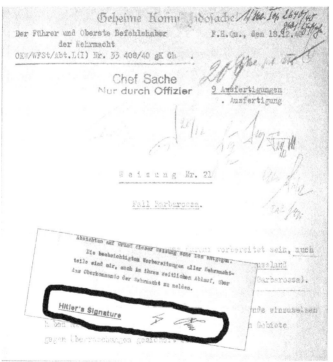

Directive No.21, signed by Adolf Hitler

Directive No. 21 Highlights²

Decades later, the US Department of the Army translated Hitler's bloodcurdling directive into English. To everyone's surprise, the directive was short and succinct, written in easy-to-understand language by Hitler himself, and formatted much like the fact-based executive summary of a corporate business plan. Since most Americans have never seen or heard of the Directive, here are a few brief sections to give a greater understanding of Hitler as Commander-in-Chief.

"The German Wehrmacht must be prepared to decisively crush Soviet Russia during Operation Barbarossa [. . .]

I.   ***Operations***

For this purpose, the Army will employ all available units to dominate ground operations [. . .]

The Luftwaffe will release such strong forces to support dominated areas and to adequately protect against all enemy air attacks [. . .]

I shall order the concentration against Soviet Russia possibly eight weeks before the intended beginning of operations. Preparations are to be started now – if this has not yet been done – and completed by May 15, 1941 [. . .]

The mass of the Russian Army in Western Russia is to be destroyed in daring operations, by driving forward deep armoured wedges, and the retreat of units capable of combat into the vastness of Russian territory is to be prevented. [. . .]
In quick pursuit, a line is then to be reached from which the Russian Air Force will no longer be able to attack the territory of the German Reich across the Volga-Arkangel line, and the

---

² Use of a parenthesis means additional content deleted. See References.

Russian Baltic Sea Fleet will quickly lose its bases and no longer be able to fight [. . .]

II.   *Allies*

Romania will support the attack of the German southern wing; pin the enemy down where German forces are not committed; and render auxiliary service in the rear area.

Finland will cover the concentration of the German North Group withdrawn from Norway [. . .]

Swedish railroads and highways will be available for the rapid advancement of the German North Group [. . .]

III.   *Resources*

The number of officers to be assigned to the Operation shall be kept as small as possible; and only to the extent required for the activity of each individual [. . .]"

With Directive 21 firmly in place, the German High Command made preparations to execute what would be Hitler's bloodiest invasion.

Chapter 2

Bloody Barbarossa

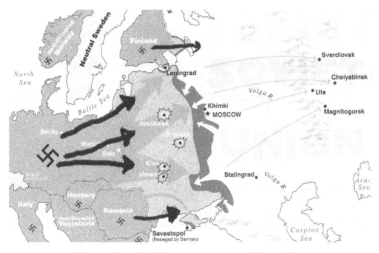

Operation Barbarossa was, and remains,
the largest military invasion in history

For reasons outside the scope of this book, Hitler held a long-standing ambition to permanently eliminate "Peasant Communism," as he privately referred to the Russian philosophy and its citizens. He wanted to annihilate the Soviet Union as a military, political, and economic power, and permanently occupy the northern cities of Archangel and Astrakhan that were rich in both oil and rare metals. In Hitler's grand scheme, the occupation of those industrial centers meant millions of Soviets would work for the Third Reich as slave laborers.

Barbarossa Begins

At about 3 A.M. on June 22, 1941, about 135 days before the Pearl Harbor attack, Hitler launched the largest and most destructive military invasion in the history of the world. Nazi Germany and its Axis powers directed 5.5 million soldiers, 3,712 tanks, 193 battleships, 47,260 howitzers and mortars, and 4,950 of the Nazi's elite Luftwaffe (air force) to invade the Soviet Union. [3]

Initially, three army groups — including more than three million German soldiers, supported by 650,000 troops from Germany's allies (Finland and Romania), and later augmented by units from Italy, Croatia, Slovakia, and Hungary — attacked the Soviet Union across a broad front. Their invasion stretched from the Baltic Sea in the north to the Black Sea in the south, and was supported by a massive number of tanks on the ground and tens of thousands of bombs, compliments of the Luftwaffe.

It is estimated that during the first few weeks of the invasion, 660,000 Soviet soldiers and citizens died and 60 percent of the Soviet Air Force was destroyed (4,017 of 7,700 aircraft), while German losses amounted to less than 150 aircraft. With much of the existing Soviet air force destroyed, Soviet ground forces were initially overwhelmed. German units encircled millions of Soviet soldiers, who were cut off from supplies and reinforcements.

Einsatzgruppen4 security police hang Soviets for sport during Operation Barbarossa

---

[3] Estimates range from 28 million to 40 million Russian soldiers and citizens died during WWII, a number greater than all the casualties of all the enemy Axis powers and all our Allies combined.

[4] Pronounced ein-za-potten. Responsible for 1.4 million deaths. See References.

Despite catastrophic losses during the first six weeks of Hitler's invasion, the Soviet Union failed to collapse as anticipated by Nazi leadership and German military commanders, and they moved many of their industries, especially war plants, east of the Urals. By the fall of 1941, Soviet resistance had stiffened as every citizen in every town went to war in one manner or another, forcing the Germans to rethink their timetable to domination. In fact, in early December the Soviet Union launched a bloody counterattack against the center of the German front, driving them back from Moscow. But Soviet offensive gains were short-lived due to a chronic lack of tanks and aircraft.

It was now clear to President Roosevelt, who only twelve months earlier had declared the Soviet Union a "dictatorship as absolute as any other dictatorship in the world," that Nazi Germany, not the Soviet Union, posed the greatest threat to the world order.

Lend-Lease Arrives

On November 1, 1941, at Roosevelt's insistence, Congress extended $1 billion (present value: $17 billion) in interest-free military aid to the Soviets under The Act to Promote the Defense of the United States, more commonly known as Lend-Lease.[5]

Initially, aid was in the form of military equipment, ammunition, consumer goods, and materials for weapons production. While such aid was useful, the Soviets continued to lose ground without major air support. By the spring of 1942, the Nazi offensive to capture the rich fields of oil and rare metals in the northern Caucasus was in full swing.

In a letter to Roosevelt, Stalin summarized his greatest need. *"We are in desperate need of supplies of modern fighter aircraft (for example, the Airacobra). The Germans have a large reserve of aircraft. In the south, the Germans have at least twice the superiority in the air, which makes it impossible for us to provide cover for our troops."*[6]

---

[5] Lend-Lease aid was either free or driven by heavily-discounted loans that were often traded for US Army and Naval bases in Allied territory.

[6] From Russian historical archives. See References in rear.

During the next two years, the US built and supplied about 22,000[7] Soviet fighter planes, while the Soviet aviation industry gradually increased its own production of fighters, bombers, and attack aircraft. Slowly, the momentum of the war was starting to shift.[8]

While the Soviets willingly accepted American military aid, Stalin and his officials publicly described this aid as a "minor factor" in winning the war. Years later, after Stalin's death, Anastas Mikoyan, the USSR's Commissar for Foreign Trade, responsible for accepting supplies from the Allies during the war, spoke candidly. "Without Lend-Lease, we would have continued fighting for another 12-18 months, and lost many more lives."[9]

American-made Soviet P-39 (Airacobra) jet fighters get final checks
at Bell Aircraft in Wheatfield, NY

---

[7] Estimates vary. Some are higher.

[8] By war's end, the P-39 had scored the highest number of individual kills attributed to any US fighter plane in the Eastern European Theatre.

[9] G. Kumanev, The People's Commissar's of Stalin Speak.

Interrupted Cargo

Despite the accelerated flow of aid, the Soviets struggled with actual delivery in the North Atlantic corridor. The heavy presence of German submarines, based primarily in Norway, disrupted everything from cargo ships to battleships. At the time, it was estimated that less than 60 percent of Lend-Lease supplies were reaching their intended destination.

Consequently, Stalin was quite intrigued by the giant US seaplane called the PBY (more commonly known as the Catalina). With modifications, he believed the plane had the multitask potential to hunt submarines, shoot down enemy aircraft, escort convoys, land troops, and rescue crews from disabled ships. To his credit, Stalin realized the Soviets lacked the engineering experience to design and maintain such a complicated aircraft. Also, only one Soviet manufacturing plant located in Beriev, Eastern Ukraine, had the infrastructure to produce a PBY-like plane. Unfortunately, that city was in German hands. And so, *Project Zebra* was born.

Chapter 3

Capitalist and Communist

*Unlikely bedfellows developed a warm relationship
at the Soviet Embassy in Tehran*

When Stalin and Roosevelt met for the first time in Tehran, Iran, in 1943, the Soviet Union was struggling with the loss of Lend-Lease war materiel in the North Atlantic. It was estimated that the German submarines, housed and maintained in Norway, destroyed 60 percent of the desperately needed Allied cargo. Another important meeting theme was agreement that the Soviets would later join the Allies and take the lead against the Japanese naval fleet in the Pacific Theater.

Mutual Interests

Stalin, Roosevelt, and ultimately Churchill realized the Soviet Navy required a substantial upgrade to achieve their primary strategic interest — the destruction of Hitler and his Nazi war machine. Privately, Stalin joked that his Naval Air Fleet might not be quite "up to the tasks at hand." During these discussions, Roosevelt saw a human side of Stalin few ever saw, and pledged to provide whatever was needed to end "this thing." [10] FDR even called Stalin "Uncle Joe" when speaking to Churchill.

Stalin candidly explained that his Naval Air Fleet consisted almost exclusively of small, two-person seaplanes called the Beriev MBR-2. Each was powered by a single engine, had a top speed of 130 miles per hour, and could remain airborne for no more than four hours. Its only armaments were two manually-loaded machine guns with no sights.

Soviet MBR-2 co-pilot and gunner
direct single-engine seaplane to landing dock

Stalin, described by a ranking American official as "a football coach's dream of a tackle with huge hands as hard as his mind," was an under-appreciated military tactician. Stalin knew what he needed: 150+ of the massive PBY's modified to Soviet war-time specifications. The Department of the Navy named this Soviet version of the PBY the PBN-1 Nomad.

---

[10] My Dear Mr. Stalin: The Complete Correspondence of FDR and Joseph V. Stalin by Susan Butler.

To receive the badly-needed Nomads as quickly as possible, Stalin temporarily agreed to forgo supplies of tanks, artillery, and ammunition. He also put his most trusted ally, Foreign Minister Vladislav Molotov, in charge of working with America to develop a complicated, high-risk plan to modify, produce, and deliver the Nomads, as well as train the crews. Committed to supporting Stalin, Roosevelt appointed a member of his military inner circle: Vice Admiral Patrick Bellinger, a distinguished Naval Air Force commander and a veteran of Pearl Harbor.

To those Americans and Soviets in charge, along with a small inner circle, the top-secret plan came to be known as *Project Zebra*. As of this writing, there are no known documentations detailing why the mission was so named. Military lore hypothesizes that the wild animal with multiple stripes was a metaphor for a freewheeling mission among multiple allies.

Circa 1944. Interim top-secret Project Zebra update

Nomad Hydraulics

Eventually, America built 185 Nomads for the Soviet Air Force. The first 25 were seaplanes that could only land and take off in water. But these custom Nomads did incorporate the latest electronics and radar.

The remaining 159 Nomads were amphibious. They incorporated state-of-the-art hydraulics and a three-wheel retractable landing gear that enabled the plane to take off and land on both water and land.

During water landings, the ends of the wings, with hollow pontoons attached, folded into a vertical position with the flick of a switch, turning the plane into a trimaran that was remarkably stable even in the choppy waters of the North Atlantic.

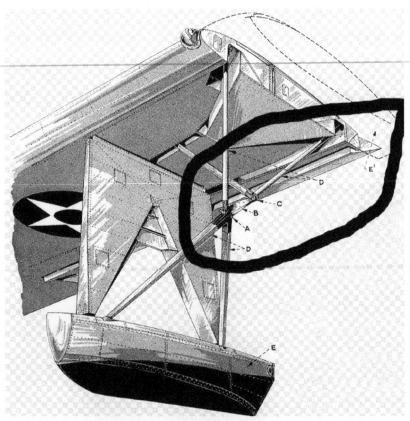

State-of-the-art Nomad hydraulics schematic

During takeoff, the Nomad glided delicately along the water and extended its wing flaps as it separated from the water. When the Nomad landed on a runway, the wings were simply lowered into a horizontal position and locked in place.

Ordnance Capacity

The Nomad contained an engine that was 50 percent more powerful than its predecessors, so it could carry a bomb load that was the equivalent to America's land-based, workhorse B-17 bombers, as well heavy-duty front and rear machine gun turrets with new, continuous-feed mechanisms.

Other design improvements included 50 percent larger fuel tanks so the plane could remain airborne at relatively low altitudes for 18-20 hours without refueling; an upgraded electrical system; multiple auxiliary emergency power back-up units; the latest radar technology; and a state-of-the-art bombsight called Norden. It required a crew of seven (two pilots, two gunners, a bombardier, a radio operator, and a flight engineer) in combat and had sleeping accommodations for three crew members during noncombat periods.

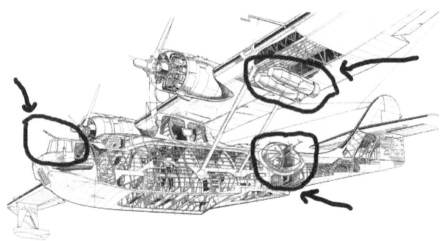

Nomad drawing shows increased ordnance capacity

Nomad Production

The consensus of the US military was that our allies would have little postwar interest in the limited-edition, highly customized model Nomad. There were also concerns that interrupting the production of P-39 planes, at both the Consolidated plant in San Diego and the Bell plant in Buffalo, could create significant downtime and inefficiencies.

Consequently, the Department of the Navy decided the only practical solution was to build the Nomads at the Navy-owned Naval Aircraft Factory (NAF) in the Philadelphia shipyards. They rationalized this production plan would ensure replacement part availability; obtain cost data for the Department's guidance in its dealings with private manufacturers; allow control of additional design modifications, if any; and deliver sufficient quantities of this battle-ready craft in order to have immediate military impact.

Within a matter of months, production lines were up and running. The planes were produced and delivered in three consecutive phases, so they could be put to use as fast as America could produce them. To fulfill the complicated production requirements, the NAF worked three shifts a day, seven days a week. The Factory even had a staff devoted to incorporating the required safety warnings and markings in Russian on the equipment, as well as giant red stars on the fuselage and tail.

During the height of production activity, an estimated 2,000 employees worked on these planes. They knew what they were doing was highly unusual, yet no one leaked a word about the mission to the press.

Soviet-bound Nomads produced in downtown Philadelphia

Practical Issues

As the planes were readied to come off the production lines, Soviet and American teams turned their focus on four remaining issues:

1. The Nomad training manuals were all written in English.
2. Where would Soviet pilots be trained to fly this massive plane?
3. How would the planes reach the Soviet Union? Stalin insisted no American could fly into Soviet airspace, and Roosevelt would not allow the Soviets to fly over American airspace
4. Who would be responsible for documenting performance; needed modifications if any; parts replacement; and general maintenance?

President Roosevelt selected the small town of Elizabeth City, North Carolina, as the "where." He had visited a few years earlier and was impressed by the warmth and patriotism of its citizens. Most importantly, he approved $2 million (present value: $35 million) to dramatically expand Coast Guard runways for future military use.

President Roosevelt visits Elizabeth City

Once Lend-Lease was in full gear, Roosevelt insisted that Project Zebra be given priority for the Russians because they were desperately in need of air support. But staying the course was not easy, given the constant barrage of warnings from his vice-president, Harry Truman; his main political adversary, Thomas Dewey; and numerous senior Pentagon officials. Even his hand-picked Ambassador to Russia, Averell Harriman, balked privately. They all feared what would happen after the war to the new technology and secret military equipment provided to the Soviets.

Roosevelt ignored them all. His priority was to rid the world of Hitler. He also felt, from his prior summits, that he could work with Stalin in the post-war world. So Project Zebra became one of Roosevelt's pet projects.

Chapter 4

Why Elizabeth City?

Elizabeth City was typical of a prosperous,
patriotic American town in the 1940s

President Roosevelt's staff had done its homework. Elizabeth City was a picturesque, patriotic Americana town of 12,000 residents who lived in white clapboard houses on tree-lined streets where the American flag proudly waved. But the town's assets also offered significant military advantages.

Four Good Reasons

Elizabeth City was conveniently located, about 300 nautical miles from the US Naval Factory in Philadelphia. Nomads could be ferried southwest over land directly to the Coast Guard base; with a skeleton crew of six people, the flight took 30 to 35 hours, depending on weather conditions. The facility already had large repair bays, training facilities, and housing, although the latter needed to be expanded to handle all the Russian and American Zebra personnel.

American crew members could easily be transported by bus to the Navy Yard and have a nice meal in Philadelphia, then pick up their planes and ferry them down the coast.

Nomad route from US Naval Factory to Elizabeth City

Secondly, Elizabeth City already had a fully functional Naval Airbase, as well as the largest Coast Guard air maintenance station in the United States. The facility had a wide, active runway and control tower, which handled a broad range of land and sea planes. It was strategically located at the end of the 22-mile long Pasquotank River, which emptied into Albemarle Sound and ultimately the Atlantic Ocean.

This discreet but accessible location and the long, wide runway ensured American crews of an additional measure of safety during nighttime flight training.

Navy-Coast Guard base and runways suited Project Zebra

This unique combination of privacy, safety, and connectivity made the base virtually undetectable by the German U-Boats actively targeting American merchant ships in the Atlantic, not far from the North Carolina's Outer Banks. And then there was the unique repair capability.

The naval base housed a giant wooden hangar used to store and repair Navy blimps that flew up and down the coast, looking for German submarines. The hangar could easily store and repair the Nomads as well.

Navy blimp hangar used for Nomad storage and repair

While residents were aware of the increased activity at the base, it would be weeks before they would meet their first Russians.

As one of Elizbeth City's long-term residents, Allen Gallop,[11] now 80, recalled, "As a kid, my friends and I used to walk over to the bay early in the morning on weekends, and watch the giant planes with a red star on the side take off and land. There was always a lot of talking, pointing, and laughing, but we were too far away to understand what they were saying. At dusk, the planes always seemed to stop flying, and we'd head home. I told Mom and Dad about what I saw. Dad would just shrug his shoulders and say, 'No business of mine.'"

---

[11] Conversations by the author with Gallop in June 2016.

Allen Gallop fondly remembers 70 years ago

The Coast Guard station was less than 50 miles away from one of the largest American naval bases in the world, Naval Station Norfolk[12]. If the American Zebra training force needed more enlisted personnel, long-range communications equipment, or specialized repairs for the Nomad's sophisticated radar and hydraulic systems, priority assistance was just a telephone call and 60 minutes away.

Zebra Trickledown

The American media — then as now — portrayed Russians as an enemy of America with designs on dominating the world. President Roosevelt fully understood the WWII détente was one of mutual survival. Privately, he told members of his inner circle that "his instincts" suggested there might be more common ground with Stalin; however, a Naval analysis concluded that the Soviet propaganda

---

[12] Naval Station Norfolk is the official Navy Department.

machine (newspapers, radio, and official communiqués) made the average Soviet citizen unable to trust anything American.

Despite ferocious skepticism, Roosevelt understood Project Zebra would be the first time in history that Russian soldiers worked side-by-side with Americans on American soil, and would have to interact with them on a person-to-person level. Project Zebra became one of Roosevelt's pet projects because he believed its successful completion would help build the war effort and achieve eventual victory.

As the Soviets became unlikely American allies, opinion surveys indicated many Americans were confused about who was friend and who was foe. This uncertainty caused concern at the military command level that worker productivity might decline at those plants manufacturing war materials for our distant allies. Consequently, the Office of War Information — with the approval of the War and State Departments — created a poster campaign that appeared on America's factory floors and store windows to clarify that issue. It was called "This man is your FRIEND." Examples follow.

"Friends" war poster campaign clarified Allied Forces

In the 1940s, there was no such thing as pre- and post-image studies, but anecdotal evidence suggests the government program did have influence.

Lifelong Elizabeth City resident Rodney Foreman, now 87, remembers: "As a teenager, Saturday was devoted to having lunch at the local Woolworth counter with my friends, followed by walking around Main and Waters Street [the town's busiest streets] looking for girls we knew from school. You couldn't help but notice the soldiers walking around in unfamiliar uniforms. One of my friends asked, 'Who are they?' I looked in a store window and saw a poster with this Russian soldier. Not thinking about it, I said, 'Oh, that's one of those Russians. He's our friend.'"[13]

---

[13] Conversations by the author with Rodney Foreman, June 2017.

Chapter 5

Rarely By-the-Book

Commander Stanley Chernack takes a break in Elizabeth City

As it turned out, everything about Project Zebra was different: there was no multi-cultural book of rules, no Plan B. Navy Lieutenant Commander Stanley Chernack, 31, thoroughly understood those realities.

Husky, broad-shouldered Stanley Chernack had a reputation for not wasting words, knowing how to get the most out of his men, and getting things done, although rarely did he work by-the-book. After the war, he recalled the mission quite simply: "The Russians needed those big amphibious Nomads, and it was my job to get those crews trained and on their way."

Stanley and his wife, Edith, were born two days apart in Boston, Massachusetts, in 1913, both to families of recent Russian immigrants. He attended Boston College. They would have two sons, Charles and Peter, and celebrate 60 years of marriage.

Before the war, the mechanically inclined Chernack was a wholesale beer distributor and a skilled amateur pilot. He left business behind to join the US Navy as an aviator in 1938. When World War II broke out, he had qualified for officers' training, but he almost flunked out by when he told his commander at the time that he was managing the men "the wrong way." He was accused of insolence and had a hearing in front of a panel of captains. Within the hour, he convinced the panel that his assessment was correct; the charges were dropped and he got promoted once, then a second time, and was stationed in the Atlantic Theater.

During that tour of duty, President Roosevelt launched both the Lend-Lease and our Soviet Union support programs. Then Roosevelt's senior adviser, Harry Hopkins, learned of Chernack's flying credentials, management abilities, Russian cultural heritage, and limited language fluency. After a few interviews with top brass, Chernack was appointed the American commanding officer for Project Zebra.

He was the ideal choice to blend two groups of seamen, enlisted men, and military pilots — who came from entirely different worlds — to work together as one. Chernack was a pragmatic manager who took pride in getting things done. Since there were no official operating guidelines regarding the Navy's role in Lend-Lease. Chernack had to organize the training and transfer of the Nomads using his own judgment.

Stanley visits wife Edith and son Peter at Narragansett home

He never talked much about his family, although he was clearly a proud husband and father. He knew there was no substitute for spending time with family, even in wartime. Chernack's wife, Edith, and the children lived full-time on Narragansett Island, off the coast of New England. It was a good lifestyle for the family: the grandparents were just a few hours away and the Naval Air Station was perfect for landing small craft with a minimum of fanfare. Whenever possible, Chernack flew to his island home for the weekend in one of the Navy's utility aircraft. His occasional flying guest was Lieutenant Gagarin.

Planes with Stars

By early 1944, Nomad production was in full swing at the Naval Aircraft Factory in Philadelphia when the phone rang at Chernack's desk. The production manager introduced himself and then started talking about "the twenty-five big planes with the red stars." He wanted to know when the planes were going to be picked up. "Can't fill the rest of the order until we get rid of these things. No more space."

Chernack realized he needed an efficient plan to take title, a plan that could be reused when additional planes came off the assembly line. He decided the safest and most efficient solution was to assign some of the officers to take title to the Nomads at the mouth of the river near the Philadelphia factory, and then fly them south to Elizabeth City. Chernack also knew that plan had to be executed on weekends so as not to disrupt the weekday Soviet training.

Larger than expected crew picks up Nomads in Philadelphia

Before they left, he gave everybody one order: "Make sure the damn hardware arrives safe and sound at the base by 1000 hours [10:00 A.M. in military speak] sharp… *Monday morning*. No AWOLs. Do we understand each other?"

Chernack also made it crystal clear "weekend Philly duty" was a privilege. "Don't care what you do in your free time, just don't embarrass the Navy or me."

First Pick-Up

Given the existing inventory backlog, Chernack decided to borrow a search-and-rescue PBN from the Coast Guard and send seven teams of six men (42 American Zebras in all) to simultaneously ferry a squadron of planes to Elizabeth City.

The Naval Aircraft Factory sat at the edge of the Delaware River on Front Street. When the plane arrived, a small powerboat with two seamen pulled alongside the huge aircraft. The two-person welcoming committee expected a crew of six or seven men. They were overwhelmed by the sight of 42 men standing on the massive wing, and radioed the factory for immediate assistance. "Sir, we have a situation here." Soon, there were three boats shuttling the Zebras to shore, where they completed the required paperwork, took official title to the aircraft, and parked them on the Delaware River for the weekend.

There are no records of how many weekend junkets there were, but it appears there was never one Zebra AWOL, and there are no reports of damaged aircraft, either on arrival in Elizabeth City or before departure to the USSR.

Chernack's Commandments
Chernack "The Commander" held five strong beliefs:
(1) Give men responsibility and they will rise to the occasion.
(2) Mission success requires critical-task delegation.
(3) There is no substitute for clarity of communication.
(4) No bullshit. Always tell it like it is and expect the same in return.
(5) Men in war need the ability to break from the war.

Chernack shares some free time with his officers and enlisted men

Chapter 6

Prince Gregory

The young US naval officer, Prince Gagarin

Imagine yourself as the American Project Zebra casting director. Your job: identify the ideal American naval officer to train a group of Russian men who spoke little to no English, and who were coming to America believing inaccurate stereotypes.

The specifications might sound something like this. "Seeking a person with a family heritage steeped in Russian history. Ideally, the great-grandson of a Russian aristocrat with the title of Prince, a world-class artist who traveled the globe drawing images that captured history for future generations. Make the Prince's son a man whose technical brilliance founded a world-famous engineering school, like Polytechnic University in St. Petersburg. Give me a tall, handsome, third generation son, an ostracized army officer who escaped a Bolshevik firing squad, joined the French Army, and ultimately migrated to America. And give that man a handsome, intellectually gifted son who was born in Germany; grew up in Paris; speaks German, French, Russian, and English; became a naturalized American citizen; and graduated from MIT."

Circa 1928 Paris. Future Lieutenant and his father

Reliable Bond

Prince Gregory Gagarin of Chevy Chase, Maryland, known at the time of Project Zebra as Lieutenant Greg Gagarin, was all that and more. In 1943, at the age of 21, he graduated from MIT (Massachusetts Institute of Technology) with a Bachelor of Science degree. He became familiar with every detail of operating and maintaining the navigational systems and radar of the Nomads that were built at the Philadelphia Naval Aircraft Factory. And he was one of the few Americans in the military who not only spoke fluent Russian and understood Russian culture and mindset, but was also trained in the new technology.

The tall naval officer with a soft-spoken sense of humor became a trusted, reliable bond that held together the secret training of over 200 Russian naval pilots and crew *in America* during a 19-month period, May 1944 to October 1945.

Engineering DNA

By Gagarin's junior year at MIT, it was becoming increasingly clear that America would be drawn into Hitler's War. German submarines were regularly sinking Allied ships in convoys across the Atlantic, as well as merchant ships along the American coastline. As Gagarin was walking through the main entrance hall of MIT one day, he passed a Navy recruitment desk. After general discussions with the officer there and with his parents, he accepted the Navy's offer of a commission as an Ensign in the US Naval Reserve, to be effective after graduation in 1943. He felt that his interest in mechanical and electrical engineering and fascination with flight best suited him for Naval Aviation.

Gregory graduated MIT about seven months after Pearl Harbor and completed his basic ROTC training in Fort Schuyler, New York. Ironically, he was then assigned to classified radar training back at MIT. From there, he was assigned to a patrol bomber squad in Charleston, Virginia, where he learned to train skeptical, experienced US pilots on the latest technology before they transferred to the Pacific Theater.

At the time of Gagarin's arrival, the most seasoned pilots in Charleston flew by sight and instinct. The new planes were outfitted with advanced radar, new communication gadgets, and unfamiliar dashboards with new dials and sticks. To a man, everyone was skeptical about the superiority of directional radar over traditional sight-based identification. Gagarin knew a real-life demonstration was the only way to change their entrenched behavior. So one day during a training flight, Gagarin went to the navigation station and adjusted the ground coordinates, making their plane 10 percent off course. As they continued to fly, the pilot realized he was off course. Gagarin explained what he did and then reset the base coordinates with the new radar control. The plane circled and followed the radar beam directly to the base.

Before long, the 22-year old was holding classes and sitting on the floor between the pilot and co-pilot during flight training. At the time, radar was this magical new directional device that, as one officer complained, "was an invisible pilot you want me to trust."

Then Gagarin faced his first major military challenge. He knew the pilots could not complete missions against the increasingly sophisticated German submarines and U-boats without extensive use of radar. So he decided to simplify the operation of radar. He took the pilots into a repair shop and turned on a fluorescent light. Then he stood in front of it. "Can you see the light?" he asked. The men said no. "But do you think it's still on?"

The men responded, "Of course."

"That's radar. You turn it on, and it works. Trust me."

The men both did and didn't. When Gagarin was on the plane, they would use it. When he wasn't, they didn't. As he found out later, some of the pilots thought the invisible beam could sterilize them.

Party Time

A few months later, his entire regiment had a final going away bash before taking off for the Pacific Theater. Many of them knew they might never see each other again, or worse still, never return at all. So, the beer and liquor flowed. The next morning — hangover and all — Gagarin was summoned to the office of his perturbed CO. "Goddamn it Gagarin, here's your new orders," he said, dropping a teletype message on his desk. It read simply, "Report to Commander Owens of the Atlantic Fleet in Norfolk." Gagarin asked for specifics. None were forthcoming other than, "We've invested a lot of time making you a major asset for the Pacific. Just get your ass on the next train."

Gagarin's Naval air regiment prepares for Pacific Theater

Gagarin arrived in Norfolk, Virginia, the following day. Upon reporting, he was told the Colonel would see him when he could. He was assigned an officer barracks and a bed. He returned for three days in a row. Finally, the Colonel was available. Their meeting was as abrupt as the one with his prior CO. "Here's your bus ticket; you've been assigned to Elizabeth City."

Finding Elizabeth City

Gagarin had never even heard of Elizabeth City. He asked the nature of the assignment and received what was becoming a familiar refrain. "What the hell do I know! An order is an order." That evening, Gagarin got off a Greyhound bus on Main Street in Elizabeth City, about 60 miles south of Norfolk. There wasn't a person on the street. Just a single cab up the block. Gagarin told the driver to take him to the Naval Air Base.

"Don't know of any air base here," the man said. "Just that Naval facility with those big blimps."

A ten-minute ride later, Gagarin addressed an armed guard at the entrance booth. "My name is Lt. Gagarin. I was told to report here."

The man smiled and saluted. "Yes sir, they're expecting you, but everything is shut down for the night. Just head to the officers' barracks; it's to the left on the other side of the tarmac."

Huge Soviet Nomad rests on the tarmac in Elizabeth City

As he walked across the tarmac, he saw for the first time a squadron of gigantic steel gray PBN-Nomad seaplanes with big Soviet stars, dual machine-gun turrets, and large bomb bays; they lined a wide runway that led to a large body of water. He smiled to himself. Now he knew why he was ordered here.

Gagarin entered the officers' quarters in his naval greens. A Russian officer with a befuddled look stood in front of a bulletin board, examining the training agenda for the week. Gagarin could tell that the man could not read English. He decided to help. He addressed the man in Russian, "Can I help you?"

The startled man replied in Russian, "Who the hell are you?" (pronounced: "kto ty takoy").

Gagarin responded with his full name and partonic (middle name), "Lt. Grigori Grigorievich Gagarin."

Different from the Rest

As each member of the Russian crew came to know Gagarin, questions arose, again, and again.

"Was your great-grandfather the famous artist Prince Gagarin?"

"Was your grandfather the Rector of Polytechnic?"

"Did your father escape the Bolshevik purge?"

"How did you come to be American?"

In time, the Russian crews realized their polite, soft-spoken team member was different from the other Americans.

Chapter 7

Zebra Airlines

Biggest, baddest commuter plane in the world

One of Gagarin's first Zebra assignments was completely unexpected.

When the first crews returned from the Naval Aircraft Factory, they told the others of their 48-hour liberty adventure. Philadelphia was a transportation hub, so those with Eastern roots scattered in pairs to New York, New Jersey, and Washington to visit family and friends. The rest, presumably, just let off a little steam or found themselves a date, or both. As one of the men explained, "Single women are wildly patriotic."

Before long, Lt. Commander Chernack had more "crew volunteers and passenger requests" than he could handle. He even heard from his old RAF roommate, Squad Leader Fry, who wanted to know the when timing of the ferry service because a few members of his team "wanted to see the Liberty Bell."

Enter Zebra Airlines

Chernack had studied Gagarin's record. He knew Gagarin was the man for the job. Chernack explained the problem and told Gagarin, "Just handle it."

The orderly Gagarin identified which aircraft were ready for pick-up in Philadelphia and then identified discrete military airfields near interesting urban areas, such as New York, Boston, and Niagara Falls. He posted a weekly first-come, first-serve crew and passenger signup sheet in all the barracks entitled "Zebra Airlines Ferry Service."

Zebra Airline Spur

With little fanfare, the lieutenant also created his personal Zebra Airlines spur service.

Gagarin's father — also named Gregory, and now a riding instructor at the elite 110-year-old Grier School for Girls in Tyrone, Pennsylvania — invited his son to spend the weekend with him.

The next evening at the Officer's Club, Gagarin and his buddy Joe Flickinger approached Commander Chernack for a weekend pass. Joe was a civilian test pilot for Consolidated Vultee Aircraft Company, which had a small office and refueling facility on the base. He taught flight basics during the week, using a single-engine, two-seat Vultee.[14] The plane was slow as molasses and barely adequate for training maneuvers, but it did have one advantage: the Vultee was fuel-efficient. You could go up the East Coast to Boston and back on a single tank of gas. And despite their military marking, they could land at small commercial airports with a minimum of fanfare from the local air traffic controllers.

---

[14] Small plane initially invented by Vultee Aircraft Company in California, which was purchased by Consolidated Aircraft before the war. The plane quickly lost favor after the war.

Putter off to Altoona in a Consolidated Vultee

Flickinger, a former school teacher, loved to fly — anywhere, anytime — and was always up for a good time.

Gagarin asked, "Up for a little weekend fun?"

"Where and when?" responded Flickinger.

"Altoona, Pennsylvania," said Gagarin.

"What could possibly be in Altoona?" Flickinger wondered. Gagarin explained he wanted to spend a little time with his dad and meet a few debutantes before they became inaccessible to "mere mortal men."

Teacher turned test pilot for Consolidated Aircraft

By Friday afternoon, the two men had landed in Altoona and taken a 20-minute cab ride to the school. It was lunchtime. Flickinger and Gagarin walked into the busy cafeteria, looking for the senior Gagarin. A few of the girls spotted them and signaled to their friends, recalled Gagarin. "Suddenly, there wasn't a sound in the room. We could feel hundreds of female eyes following two strapping uniformed naval officers casually walking toward the instructors' table. My dad couldn't stop smiling as he introduced me to his peers, and then to several students who had circled round."

339 acres, 322 students, 72 teachers = expensive, exclusive

Flickinger's recollection was slightly different. He looked around the room and saw a bunch of teenage girls screeching. So instead of a hot date with a debutante, he was resigned to spending the evening with Gagarin, his father, and a bottle of scotch by a fireplace.

Au Fu's Icon

As the three men sat and talked about the war and politics, Flickinger noticed a tattered metal icon around the senior Gagarin's neck. He asked what it was. Gagarin Sr. said it was a "reminder of the old country."

He went on to explain how before the Bolshevik Revolution, he and his family had an enterprising business in grains. But when the

Bolsheviks came to power, he was singled out for no apparent reason and placed in a cold, dark jail cell with two other men, with three small boards for sleeping on the floor and one meal a day, for two weeks. During the middle of the night, there was a sudden banging on the door. The men were removed from the cell and told they would be taken to the court and given their releases.

They were surrounded by about eight guards with rifles as they walked down the dimly-lit cobblestone street. Gagarin knew the courthouse was to the left, but they were ordered to turn right. Gagarin believed they were about to be shot by a firing squad, and he decided it would be better to die attempting to flee. He pushed the rear guards aside and began to run. Two bullets entered his left-hand, smashing bones and causing intense bleeding.

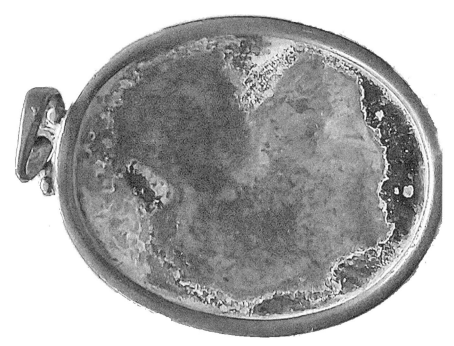

The Russian icon that altered history

As he turned the corner and headed into complete darkness, he felt something pop on his chest. There was no time to find out what.

He continued to run through fields and woods until there were no more soldiers. Eventually, he found refuge in a kind farmer's home some miles away. There, they tended to his wounds and discovered a dented religious icon once given to him by his mother. It was only then that Au Fu (a nickname he would receive from his grandchildren many years later) realized the icon had saved his life by acting as a shield against a soldier's bullet.

Airline Growth

Awareness of Flickinger and Gagarin's weekend jaunts spread. Before long, Zebra Airlines had the same problem as the Zebra Bus Company: there were more weekend requests than they could handle.

While Gagarin wanted to help everybody on the usual first come-first-serve basis, Flickinger, as the chief pilot, was more discriminating. If the trip sounded like he could have some fun, he signed up. If the trip sounded like a boring visit to a grandparent, he always had a plausible excuse.

Chernack, aware of what was going on, was a good sport. So long as there were no problems or complaints, he simply looked the other way. It was well known he made more than a few personal to visits to Edith and the kids on Narragansett.

Chapter 8

Soviet Chief No. 1

Chernack welcomes Soviet Major Pesharov to America

On April 3, 1944, the first group of 10 Soviet crews led by Major Pesharov[15] arrived in Elizabeth City. To Chernack's surprise, they arrived in heavy, dark wool uniforms. By the time the crews had disembarked and received an orientation in Russian, the sweat was pouring off their brows. Nobody complained or squirmed.

Two weeks later, on April 17, 15 more crews arrived along with a communications officer named Major Ivan Salnikov and a new commanding officer named Colonel Viktor Vassiliev, who assumed command of all 25 crews and support staff and relieved Major Pesharov of his duties. The new arrivals were wearing lighter uniforms more appropriate to the Elizabeth City spring-summer climate!

---

[15] Part II Classified U.S. Navy Narrative, September 26, 1946. See References.

Nothing is known about why the Soviet leadership changed so early in the Zebra mission.

Recognition of Vassiliev in official Naval documents

According to available Soviet historical documents, Vassiliev was considered an outstanding pilot, and was deputy commander of an elite aviation regiment prior to the years of the Great Purges.[16]

---

[16] The mid 1930's in Russia when a paranoid Stalin executed or imprisoned over 80 percent of his military officers to weed our traitors and spies.

Rehabilitated and Assigned

For unknown reasons, Vassiliev became a victim of Stalin's terror purges and was incarcerated for a number of years in a labor camp (Gulag). Unlike many of his fellow military officers, he survived. In fact, after being successfully "rehabilitated," the State appointed him Deputy Commander of the highly respected 117th Regiment, reporting to the highly-regarded officer Major Maxim Chibisov. The surprising appointment raised eyebrows within the 117th, but Chibisov welcomed him as ordered. Normally, when officers were released from rehab camp, they were given a reduction in rank and remained under the watchful eye of a state security agency. For whatever reason, this was not the case with Colonel Vassiliev.

According to Vassiliev's personnel file, he served in the 117th with "duty and honor." Three years later he was informed that he was selected to lead "a military mission of great importance to Comrade Stalin." Neither he nor Chibisov received specifics.

Three weeks later, Vassiliev alone learned he would train a handpicked group of elite pilots and crews to fly a large, deadly naval aircraft designed and produced in America. He was surprised to learn that 150+ of these aircraft were currently being designed and produced in America to Soviet modifications, and that he would train his crews in Elizabeth City, North Carolina, a place no Soviet military officer could even find on a map. He also learned there were no detailed drawings of the aircraft, no operating manuals, and no detailed training protocols. His instruction was simple and clear: "one of your important duties will be to agree on a training process with the Americans that reflects proudly on the Soviet people and Soviet war efforts."

First Crews

The initial 25 Soviet crews to Elizabeth City included a pilot and co-pilot; two navigators; an engineer; an electronics officer; and communication, ordnance, and maintenance specialists. None of the men spoke or understood English which, according to the Naval commanders, "made their training very difficult."

Initial Elizabeth City Soviet arrivals personally welcomed

Ten crews came from the North Atlantic Fleets, ten from Far East Fleets, and five from the Black Sea Fleet. The apparent goals: reopen the North Atlantic corridor, at that time dominated by German U-boats; support Pacific Theatre operations against the Japanese; and protect Russian Black Sea battleship access.

Each crew arrived in a different fashion. Vassiliev and the North Atlantic crews arrived on British military aircraft from Murmansk to England to Norfolk, Virginia (60 miles by bus from Elizabeth City). The Pacific crews traveled to Krasnoyarsk, Siberia, by passenger train and then to Fairbanks, Alaska, on commercial airline flights. The Black Sea crews flew to Murmansk and then traveled directly to Norfolk by sea.

When Vassiliev walked through the gates of the US Coast Guard station in Elizabeth City, he saw 25 enormous Nomads with red stars sitting on the runways and parked around the hangars. He and the crews walked around the planes, aghast. They had previously flown only two-passenger, single-engine seaplanes.

They were given a brief tour of the complicated cockpits, communication and navigation equipment, and huge storage bays and then introduced to their quarters. The Russian officers were co-mingled with their American counterparts in all common areas to improve communication and partnership. The enlisted men were assigned a Soviet-only barracks since none spoke English.

The early recollections of Vassiliev among the American command were that he was quiet and plain-spoken, but had the absolute respect of every man under his command. He never raised his voice, never had a command challenged, and was courteous to every American he met.

Vassiliev was also acutely aware of the military *and* public relations importance of Project Zebra. In addition to being involved in every aspect of the training, he spent significant time on daily calls to the Russian Embassy in Washington. In those days, calls needed to be placed by a communications specialist. That task fell to Lt. Gregory Gagarin — one of the only Americans who spoke flawless Russian. As Gagarin recalled, "Vassiliev's conversations covered specific training process and progress and his observations on the crew's daily interactions with the Americans. I think he forgot I could understand what he said, but never once did I hear a disparaging comment."

Solving Problems

Vassiliev didn't like surprises. To him, a job well done meant that things went smoothly. Because of Gagarin's practical engineering background, princely Russian heritage, and mechanical aptitude, he quickly became Vassiliev's go-to guy. A familiar refrain heard in the officers' quarters was, "So, Mr. Gagarin, what are we going to do about this problem?"

Vassiliev was accustomed to the Russian way: everything done by the book. But Gagarin knew the entire Zebra project was unchartered and unique — there was no book. So, on his own, he'd make up something that sounded plausible and then see if his solutions worked. Sometimes they did, and sometimes they didn't. But as Gagarin recalled, "Somehow, we always found a reasonable solution."

When Vassiliev thought a solution sounded too far-fetched, he'd simply ask, "Mr. Gagarin, are you sure? You could have a comedic opera on your hands."

That comment led Gagarin to believe the Napoleonic Vassiliev might have more of a sense of humor than previously assumed. One evening at the Club, Gagarin suggested some of Vassiliev's officers might want to reserve a seat on Zebra Airlines to see some of the American sights. Vassiliev's response, "Soviet soldiers do not take weekend holidays during wartime."

Burning Mattress

In keeping with his personality, Vassiliev was a quiet disciplinarian. One evening, one of his officers got drunk while smoking in bed and the mattress caught fire. A serious fire was quickly averted thanks to pails of water dumped on the mattress by the other enlisted men. Vassiliev was embarrassed and furious with the officer. "In Russia, this man would be shot for such behavior," he said.

Vassiliev's American counterpart, Chernack, agreed the behavior was unacceptable, but he wasn't sure if Vassiliev was serious about the "shot" comment, so he calmly explained that was not the American way. "We need to find a more appropriate solution." Vassiliev ordered the man to sleep in the burnt, wet bed for three days before allowing the American quartermaster to issue him a replacement mattress. He also stationed a guard outside the barracks, 24 hours a day, to make sure the man didn't cheat.

After the Soviet officer's next flight to Russia, he never returned.

History Documented

May 1944. Chernack informed Vassiliev that the Navy Department was coming down to take a few historic photos of the entire group of Americans and Russians before anybody left on the first trip to Russia. Vassiliev knew such historic pictures might become part of his legacy. He wanted things to be perfect. He made sure his entire crew was dressed in their neatest, cleanest uniforms. Vassiliev used to say, a "well dressed soldier is a respected soldier."

While the official photographers waited, Vassiliev organized and reorganized his crews by rank, by time in the service, and by whatever means he thought important. He even placed the Americans where he thought they should go.

Original Naval photo of American trainers and Soviet teams

The Colonel also assumed that this group photo would one day appear in Soviet publications, so he had a second group picture taken. He wanted the Russian contingent to be more prominent. The Americans were happy for him to have his way in the second picture. Comparing the two pictures, the one for Soviet consumption had fewer American trainers. There is one constant in both: Vassiliev is dead center.

Vassiliev's preferred version; note reduction of American officers

Going Home

By the end of June 1944, Vassiliev's first crews had been trained and given specific flight orders.

Because of the urgent need to disrupt German dominance of the North Atlantic, all 25 Nomads would take the shortest possible route with the assistance of American and British crews. American crews flew the first leg up the Eastern Seaboard to Gander, Newfoundland. From there, British pilots flew the planes to Reykjavik, Iceland. Finally, Soviet pilots would complete the final leg, landing in the northern Russian city of either Murmansk or Arkangel, about 370 miles further east. The 4,500-mile flight took a total of about 25-30 hours, depending upon speed and wind direction.

Original Zebra North Atlantic Route, June-September 1944

Once in Russia, maintenance crews prepared the planes for battle by attaching four 1,000-pound bombs under the wings, 2,000 pounds of depth charges secured to the base of the fuselage, and thousands of 50-calibre machine gun rounds in the cargo bay.

Lone Caveat

While the North Atlantic route was most direct, it was also understood to be the most dangerous. German planes circled the northern coast of Norway night and day, hunting Allied convoys.

Knowing that, and knowing the fact that they would not be carrying a full payload of ordnance, Commander Vassiliev's crews practiced flying at low altitude (sometimes only 30 feet above the water) in both day and night conditions over the sound and ocean near the Elizabeth City base. However, the training had a limitation: there was no way to simulate the craggy peaks of Norway's rugged coastline.

Chapter 9

On-the-Job Training

Vassiliev (right front) and two Russian officers (white hats) discuss on board flight training issues with American counterparts (khaki shirts)

Vassiliev took great pride in being well prepared for the "possible." He divided his personnel into six detachments of similarly qualified pilots and specialists so they could contribute to any Nomad crew, regardless of their origination or destination. He also believed traditional Soviet aviation protocol was important, i.e., each crew member should be familiar with all the plane's fundamentals in case emergencies arose.

Vassiliev pushed and pushed. He wanted each crew — within 20 days of arrival in Elizabeth City — to be ready to ferry the aircraft, confident in the belief that every onboard element had been tested and was in working order. The more he learned about the Atlantic Ocean's weather and wind conditions, the more insistent he became about each pilot completing two six-hour training flights over the Atlantic, to become familiar with conditions they might encounter while flying from Iceland to Murmansk.

Vassiliev also studied real-time battle reports from Canada which indicated that these flying boats were most effective when they avoided German detection before dropping ordnance. He asked the American training team to place greater emphasis on flying in blind conditions, and whenever possible to fly into cloud formations, the darker the better. He also asked them to practice course identification based on silent radio beacons, and to use radio than verbal communiqués.

This on-the-job-style training worked well. Usually, after the third full day of flight training, the attentive and resourceful Soviet pilots could fly the planes on their own, with Americans acting as backup support that only intervened in extreme cases.

Casual Surprise

In the early days of training, there were two surprises. First, Vassiliev and the Soviet crews discovered the American experts seemed to have a "casual" approach to aviation.

Soviet engineers were accustomed to handling their own engine maintenance, including flushing radiators, lubricating parts, etc. They were astonished to find that the US engineers never opened the engines and had no idea where most engine components were located. Through interpreters, the Americans tried to explain the difference between flight crews and ground engineering maintenance.

Gagarin tried to explain the American philosophy of departmental responsibility. The concept did not translate easily, partly because the American words had no exact Russian translations, and partially because the Russians simply did not have the wartime resources to separate such functions.

Operating Manual Surprise

The second problem: all the operating manuals were in English only. From that point forward, Gagarin's unique vocabulary skills and flight knowledge made his involvement a 24-hour-a-day necessity.

Soviet planes, particularly the two-person seaplanes, contained a minimum of technology. Seaplane pilots had no formal training classes and no prior experience with techniques like switching engines in midair, or with the use of modern navigation systems and autopilot devices. The pilots were accustomed to receiving only a brief orientation of the plane's functions and taking a few practice flights.

The enormous Nomad dashboards had more instrument dials than any that the Soviets had ever seen, much less used. Gagarin would sit in the middle on the floor, flanked by a Soviet pilot on the right and the American instructor pilot on his left. The instructor would shout step-by-step commands over the engine noise, and Gagarin would figure out, in a matter of seconds, how to translate the instructions and related instrument readings into a simple directive the Russian pilot could understand.

Restricted use Nomad training manuals

"The process was intense, but had its lighter moments," said Gagarin. "I recall a Soviet pilot was performing his first night landing on the sound. He descended too fast. The American pilot screamed to pull up rather than crash. It happened so quickly; the Soviet pilot didn't understand my entire communication. The American pilot went nuts, pounding on the dashboard, and waving skyward. The Soviet pilot nodded affirmatively, remained calm as we gingerly bounced off a few waves, and then turned the nose of the plane skyward." [17]

Advanced Nomad navigational systems
were unknown in the Soviet Union at the time

On land or in the air, Gagarin quickly learned that many basic electronic and radar terms simply didn't translate. The fact that the Nomads carried the latest and most sophisticated navigational aids didn't help. So, Gagarin and the Russians who spoke a bit of English worked hard at common translations. For example, a 60-cycle frequency (the rate per second at which current changes direction)

---

[17] Diaries and logbooks, Lt. Gregory Gagarin. See References.

was eventually explained as the word *chis-tota* (moves back and forth quickly).

Over time, communication would take two steps forward and one step backward as each party learned a bit of the other's vocabulary. The result: communication issues were more quickly remediated, and training sessions became more productive. The rigid, conservative Vassiliev, not accustomed to dealing with uncertainty, remained calm and professional throughout this roller-coaster learning process.

During the Zebra mission, Vassiliev occasionally showed a sense of humor. One day, before the plane took off with Gagarin in his usual position, Vassiliev boarded the plane carrying a large canvas bag. "Men wanted you to have as thank you," smiled Vassiliev. Gagarin opened the bag: it contained two pillows for him to sit on.

Hole in the Dashboard

If you look closely at the picture on page 68 you will see a space, circled in white, for a piece of equipment to be secured to the dashboard. The Nomads were built with a state-of-the-art navigational aid for landing at bases during night flights. The approximately 8" by 8" space held a powerful signal receiver designed to pick up signals from ground airport transmitters. Each possible airport in the United States had a specific code (not unlike today's airport codes), allowing the pilot to accurately target where he was trying to land.

After the planes were produced, the American designers discovered that Russian airports had no transmitter capability or equipment. The hole was just left alone, rather than spending time and money on adding something of so little practical use to the Soviets. Besides, the Americans rationalized, not having the heavy receiver left more available weight to carry ammo and bombs.

Vassiliev asked what the hole was. Gagarin explained, but Vassiliev's body language told him the Commander didn't believe him. Gagarin explained it was all in the manual. Vassiliev was unimpressed. "English only." Gagarin showed him the drawing of the instrument panel in the manual. "More English." Gagarin just let things pass.

*Secret hole in the panel as it routinely appeared
in every Nomad operations manual*

Later that evening, Gagarin accidentally overheard Vassiliev speaking to some of his officers in Russian. "He explained he was pretty certain the space held a secret device that only the Americans were authorized to use."

Faulty Radio

Following the final test flights, a delivery and acceptance statement was drawn up to include all the property associated with the first 25 Nomads, and it was signed by all relevant parties. Two days before the departure date, the navigators received maps and the latest information on prevailing winds and ascending and descending air currents so they could create a route that included main and alternate airfields, emergency landing areas, and the locations of radio beacons and directional finders.

Despite being well-prepared, nature created issues for some of the first flights to the North Atlantic theater. They encountered poor weather conditions, including thick Arctic clouds which caused a dangerous icing on the wings. As one of the first pilots wrote in his diary,

> *"We flew at perhaps 40 meters over the stormy seas using only our radar altimeter settings. My navigator suggested we turn on the autopilot. I remember thinking this was the first time we used such technology during an actual mission. Unknown at the time, my flight navigator had made an error with compass bearings. Two hours before landing in Reykjavik, he realized his error, 'Captain, we passed Iceland some time ago.'"*

The British pilot saw the problem. He looked at the fuel gauge and attempted to explain the need to turn around before they ran out of fuel. But none of the Soviet crew spoke English. The Brit needed to solve the problem quickly. He sent an urgent radiogram to Reykjavik. Minutes later a British fighter plane caught up to the Nomad and signaled for it to follow the fighter back to the base.

Gagarin recalled there were also mechanical bugs in those first flights. As a Russian crew prepared to take off from Newfoundland, the pilot complained in Russian to Gagarin, who was sitting on the floor next to him, "Faulty radio, don't work."

Gagarin did an interior equipment check; everything seemed to be in working order, despite the pilot's transmission complaint. He then began to inspect the plane's exterior. He quickly noticed that the copper antenna wire that stretched from the front of the plane to the rear tail had broken free from the grommets attached to the plane's fuselage.

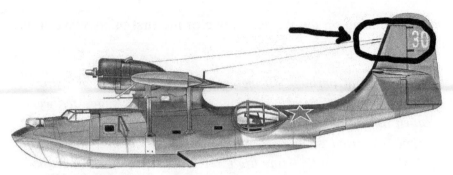

Diagram indicates placement of suspect radio transmission antenna

His simple solution: replace the copper antennae with a new, longer one that could be threaded through the grommet and soldered in place. The pilot later reported that the radio performed flawlessly during flight. In his subsequent report Gagarin noted the design flaw and his fix, and all future Nomad radio antennas produced in Philadelphia were designed similarly.

Chapter 10

The Spy Among Us

Инженер-полковник
В.В. Терциев

Штурман авиагруппы
майор А. Шапкин

Инженер
майор П.И. Турмилов

Капитан
В. Федоров

Инженер-майор
И.Н. Сальников

Полковник
М.Н. Чибисов

Which Russian Zebra officer was the spy among us?

The American training crew assumed the Soviets would arrive with a member of Russian counterintelligence cleverly disguised as a Zebra Mission senior officer. To avoid potential issues, the American Zebras — none of who had ever visited the USSR — received extensive briefings about Russia's three main counterintelligence organizations. They were also introduced to Stalin's latest espionage brainchild: SMERSH (i.e., Spetsialnye MEtody Razoblacjeniya

SHpionov); which roughly translated meant *Special Methods of Spy Detection.*

SMERSH Mandate

In practice, SMERSH had become the umbrella organization for all three Soviet counterintelligence agencies and it reported directly to Stalin, so he could closely monitor all possible anti-Soviet activities. While SMERSH initially focused on subverting German infiltration activities, Stalin quickly expanded its role to seek and punish "anti-Soviet elements," investigate traitors and deserters, and thoroughly vet Soviet military and civil personnel returning from captivity. SMERSH became so influential that Stalin had a logo and posters created to publicize its ubiquitous presence to friend and foe alike.[18]

SMERSH poster looked like a Madison Avenue ad campaign

SMERSH Zebra

While there is no documentation that a SMERSH operative was attached to Zebra, the manner in which one member of the Soviet Zebra team operated suggested otherwise.

---

[18] SMERSH: Stalin's Secret Weapon. Dr. Vadim Birstein, Biteback Publishing, 2013

"Outwardly, Ivan Salnikov, if that was his name, was introduced as Chief of Communications and Chief of Staff. Salnikov seemed to be a pleasant, easygoing officer who spoke softly," recalled Gagarin. "But he seemed different from the others — his presence was unpredictable. He came in and out of training classes at will and never flew training missions. He was party to all calls to the Russian Embassy in Washington and always seemed to accompany the Soviet Zebra crew members when they visited Elizabeth City.

"Surprisingly, Ivan spoke very little English, so when he was present at Zebra Headquarters, he mostly watched what they did, and made notes.

"At the end of each training day, he appeared to hold debriefing sessions with individual crew members and work closely with Vassiliev. We had no idea at the time, that Vassiliev had been rehabilitated," recalled Gagarin. "Ivan seemed well-liked by Soviet Zebras. I never observed or even sensed any personal tensions. But then again, the Soviets always kept their emotions in check. We used to joke privately: these guys must have ice in their veins from all the chilled vodka."

Southern Hospitality

Late one Friday afternoon, Vassiliev made a surprise announcement to his staff. He thanked the officers for their hard work and said anyone who would like to visit Elizabeth City over the weekend would be free to accompany Ivan. About eight or so officers decided to take advantage of the "escorted" R&R.

The first volunteer was the mild-mannered head of procurement, Lt. Col. Boris Tiertsiev, who spent much of his time preparing and reviewing financial reports with the Russian Embassy in Washington. Tiertsiev appeared to know about every plane part, nut, bolt, and screw sold to Russia. His job was to make sure the Americans did not cheat. As Commander Chernack indicated in his notes, "Tiertsiev was the perfect numbers man: he never smiled."[19]

---

[19] Records of Stanley Chernack. See References.

It was a hot, humid weekend when the men arrived in town wearing their uniforms and boots. After window shopping for a few hours, the men needed some cool refreshments. Ivan noticed a town landmark, the Apothecary Shop, a few blocks down East Main Street. He had learned the American word "soda."

Soviet Zebras get a taste of refreshing southern hospitality

The Apothecary Shop, opened in 1915 by Sidney Etheridge, was like something out of a Norman Rockwell painting. The rear wall was filled with jars of colorful candies sold by the piece or pound. The front of the counter had 16 flavors of ice cream in a refrigerated cabinet with a clear glass top. Each flavor had a neat card describing the content of each tub. The Russians had never seen anything like the Apothecary Shop. Salinkov began to talk to the man behind the counter in some version of English. He had no idea it was Sidney himself. Sidney patiently explained how the counter system worked. Ivan nodded, and then explained in Russian to his men that they were to point to the flavor they wanted, and the man would put a scoop in a sugar cone. They salivated in anticipation.

The first officer pointed. Sidney asked, "One scoop or two?" The officer looked at an equally perplexed Salnikov. "Two," replied Salnikov, because it was easier to pronounce. The officer's eyes almost popped out of his head in delight when a cone with two scoops of ice cream arrived. Minutes later, all the men were eating two-scoop cones, laughing and smiling as they twirled around on the stools at the counter.

Sidney was curious. "Where you boys from?"

Salnikov responded, "Russia."

"Ain't never gonna get there," replied Sidney, "but been reading about the way you boys are pushing that Nazi guy around. Thank you for your efforts."

Salnikov explained what Sidney had said. They all held up their cones and toasted Sidney in Russian, "Vast-troy-via."

Sidney smiled. "Same to you."

Salnikov asked how much the men owed. Sidney replied simply. "Awww, forget it. The cones are on me. Least I could do for *our* war effort."

Salnikov was totally unprepared for Sidney's generosity. It was not what he had been taught to expect from Americans. He returned to the base and relayed the story to Vassiliev, who relayed it to Gagarin. From that moment forward, the Russian officers were free to visit downtown Elizabeth City without an escort. However, the rank-conscious Vassiliev did not give his enlisted men the same privilege.

Never on Sunday

By the 1940s, the cult of Stalin had replaced churches with religious icons. Propaganda was everywhere in the form of pictures and statues, and history textbooks had been changed to make Stalin the unquestioned hero of the Revolution while obliterating the names of people who had been purged. Mothers taught their children that Stalin was the wisest man of the age.

An unwanted visitor stops by Zebra headquarters

One Saturday afternoon, two bearded Russian Orthodox priests, in long black robes and with big crosses hanging around their necks, walked into the Zebra World Headquarters. Some of the Americans pilots were playing cards and having a few beers. The Priests said they had heard that there were some Russians visiting the community. The pilots called Gagarin over.

Gagarin greeted them in Russian. They were surprised at his fluency, given his US Navy uniform. "Sir, we thought we might preform a Sunday service on base for the Russian soldiers."

Gagarin spoke to Chibisov, who hesitated. He explained he had to check with his staff. Shortly after that, Gagarin saw Chibisov talking to Salnikov and Tiertsiev. Chibisov returned and said, "Tell them thanks, but no thanks. I feel the crew needs to complete some additional training on Sunday."

The priests were not surprised when Gagarin returned and replied, "The men couldn't make it; they have training exercises. Another time, perhaps?"

The priest smiled knowingly. "There is a saying going around Russia: 'When citizens are in nee,d they should come to Stalin first and God later, but only if it is necessary.'"

The priests never came by again.

Who was the Spy Among Us?

Chernack had been briefed on the Soviet way. He knew Vassiliev had spent some time being rehabilitated, and assumed the Russian Zebras included one, or perhaps two, SMERSH operatives.

Chernack and Gagarin assumed the lead operative was the timid-looking, forty-something Colonel Tiertsiev. As the Soviet's chief procurement officer, Tiertsiev always seemed to be writing reports and making trips to both the Philadelphia Naval Aircraft Factory and the Russian Embassy in Washington, D.C. Chernack was certain his official role was a convenient cover for him to discuss the progress and problems of the Project Zebra mission with his superiors. In addition, there was virtually nothing about Tiertsiev as a person in his official file: no family background, no military history other than a few commendations for meritorious service.

Tiertsiev looks like a man with secrets

The younger, more congenial Salnikov's background was more readily available and appeared rather normal. He was about 32 at the time of Zebra. He was born in a small village called Kulnevo, and he worked at a local grain mill until he entered the military in the late 1930s. He apparently fought with distinction as a member of the Soviet Air Force Black Sea fleet as they battled the Germans to retain control of the Ukraine and Crimea. [20]

---

[20] Papers of Ivan Nikolayevich Salnikov, see References.

Friendly counter-intelligence operative, Major Salnikov

Whenever he wasn't in Washington, Tiertsiev seemed to be in a private one-on-one discussion with Salnikov. "Didn't matter to us," said Gagarin. "We had a job to do. Whatever they yakked about was their business."

Open Invitation

One day, Major Salnikov approached Gagarin to take a walk, to discuss "certain engineering issues." Gagarin was surprised since Salnikov had previously shown little interest in the Nomad's actual operation. As they walked and talked in Russian, Salnikov explained "they" were impressed with his unique combination of skills and his scientific background, and the fact that he knew about all the three most important facets of plane operations — engineering, electrical, and mechanical.

"After the war, we could find a very good job for you in *your* Homeland. Maybe at your grandfather's Polytechnic. Life would be very pleasant."

Gagarin paused. "Russia is my heritage, not my Homeland. You guys tried to kill my father. He fled rather than be shot. Remember?"

Salnikov paused. "That was a long time ago. Things are different. We don't do that now."

Gagarin had no interest. But he also realized it best to be polite for the sake of the mission. He replied simply, "let me think about it." Salnikov understood. He never tried to recruit Gagarin again.

Gagarin reported the conversation to Chernack. They agreed that "the real spy among us" was the friendly, smiling Major Salnikov.

Unsubstantiated rumors then circulated that Salnikov was significantly older than 32, and that he had been a Soviet counterintelligence agent for almost 20 years. No documents were found to support that statement, nor are there any records available that indicate where Salnikov was assigned after the completion of Project Zebra.

Chapter 11

R.I.P. Over Norway

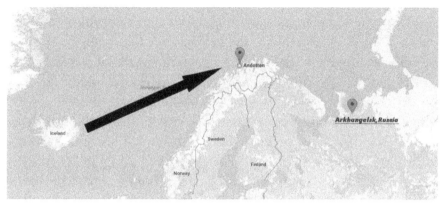

Andotten peaks at the northern tip of Norway where
Vassiliev and crew perished

Soldiers in harm's way maintain staunch loyalty to their fellow soldiers. Viktor Vassiliev was one such officer. In the end, that loyalty proved to be fatal.

Engine Failure

June 22, 1944. The last of the first group of 25 Nomads had refueled and were ready to leave Iceland.

Shortly after takeoff, the Nomad under the command of Captain Igor Boychenko experienced engine failure and was forced to return to Reykjavik. Vassiliev and his co-pilot Colonel Boris Mosuyepan, who were readying for takeoff, decided to remain on the ground until repairs were made. Because of the known concentration of German activity in the North Atlantic, they believed it would be safer to fly in tandem.

According to Boychenko's subsequent report, as he and Vassiliev approached the craggy Norwegian coastline, dotted with 4,000-foot peaks,[21] they encountered thick, dark fog. Vassiliev decided the conditions would make it virtually impossible to spot enemy aircraft, so he ordered radio silence until both were safely inside Soviet airspace.

In what would be his final transmission from Aircraft No. 25, Vassiliev reported that his plane was flying at a course of 66 degrees and an altitude of 500 meters, and he could see the enemy U-boats in the water below them. Boychenko's reading suggested Vassiliev had flown significantly off course. He saw Vassiliev's plane heading toward one of the peaks. Boychenko broke silence, shouting "Rise ahead, rise ahead." But it was already too late. Suddenly, there was nothing *but* silence. Boychenko had no choice but to continue to his destination. Hours later, he and his crew arrived safely in Murmansk. They waited for hours in the hangar, hoping, but Vassiliev, Mosuyepan, and their crew never appeared.

As the war permitted, Soviet and British crews searched the area unsuccessfully for seven days (June 23-30, 1944). The official Soviet report concluded that when Boychenko broke radio silence, German radar identified the plane's location and sent a squadron to down the struggling Nomad.

The American version of what happened differed. "It is believed to make up for lost time, Colonel Vassiliev attempted to by-pass Murmansk and land directly in Moscow."[22]

---

[21] 70 percent of the Norwegian coastline is comprised of rugged mountains rising abruptly from the sea. This is particularly true off the North Coast were 80 islands hold towering peaks 4,000 feet high and taller.

[22] Part II Classified U.S. Nay Narrative, September 26, 1946. See References.

German U-boats parked in Norway

Unofficial rumors persisted. Some officers suggested the plane's flight information had been compromised by traitors in the Soviet ranks, so the German squadron was waiting for them.

This unsubstantiated rumor gained traction with the increasingly paranoid Stalin, who issued a new directive. All crew members who participated in Project Zebra from that point forward were forbidden to send news of their mission to their relatives. Thy was allowed only one notation: "I'm alive, well, and serving." And even that mail was routed through the Soviet military channels, so there would be no hint of the note's origin. From that moment on, anyone who participated Project Zebra was like a *missing person* to their families.

Northern Reroute

Vassiliev's demise had other consequences for Project Zebra. The Nomad's direct Pacific Ocean-Iceland delivery route was shut down and replaced by a longer, more circuitous North-through-Alaska flight plan, which was both good and bad. The route was well charted. Thousands of American P-39 fighter planes had been successfully delivered to the Soviet Air Force that way without incident.

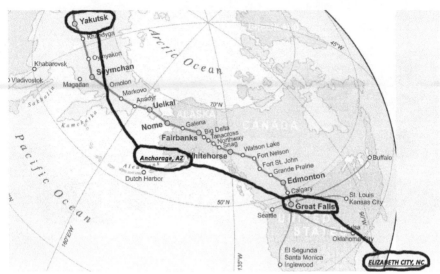

Nomads' Northern air route traveled across the US,
through Alaska, and on to Siberia

However, as the war progressed, so did Stalin's well-documented spies-are-everywhere paranoia. Consequently, he forbade Americans from flying over Soviet airspace or landing on Soviet soil. Not surprisingly, America responded in kind. Soviet crews were not allowed to fly or assist in in the delivery of Nomads when they traveled in American air space.

The effect of these tit-for-tats was an awkward, inefficient process. The Americans would fly the planes to New Orleans, Louisiana; San Diego, California; and finally, to Kodiak, Alaska, a military base on an island off the southern part of the state. The Soviet crews were flown separately to Kodiak via American military transport. Once the Soviets crews boarded the Nomads, they were authorized to use one flight route: due north, regardless of weather conditions. The planes had to make an additional refueling and maintenance stopover in Anchorage, Alaska, before the Soviets took title and flew to Yakutsk, Siberia, making additional fuel stops along the way on Soviet soil. This more convoluted trip covered 6,500 miles and could take up to 14 days, depending on flight conditions and the number of fueling stops required in remote places like Ulekal, Markovo, and Anadyr.

Hanging Chad

Sixty-three years after Commander Vassiliev's death in 1944, the remains of a badly damaged and rusted Soviet flying boat was found by 188th Norwegian Reconnaissance Regiment near the steep cliffs of Andotten, Norway. According to their 2007 report, the plane had no bullet holes, no war-related damage. Just bits of uniforms with skeletal decay and miscellaneous log books.

Consolidated PBN-1 "Nomad" Andotten South Island

118 RAP (Reconnaissance Aviation regiment) VVS SF SNO 02826 **6.17 1944**

The a / c was on a transfer flight from Canada via Iceland two Murmansk When it hit the steep cliffs of Andotten early in the morning due two heavy fog. The airplane had Russian crew some high ranking officers. All six on board were killed in the crash. Colonel / Polkovnik **Nikolaj Romanov** , Colonel / Polkovnik **Viktor Vasilev** . Ivan Mostsepan . Anatoliy Skvortsov . Nikolay Kuznetsov . K. Tjitjkan .

Andotten

It was kl 06 00 that the plane belonged to the Northern Fleet 118 Reconnaissance Aviation regiment (118 RAP VVS went into the steep cliff

It is said that it was littered with luxury items from America, nylon stockings, clothes and chocolate engine mountainside. The Germans removed the wreck and got taken down the omkomne Tidflog able to the local boat from Andotten to be saved. An airplane wing lay long side of the mountain as a memento of the event. If the plane had gone from 15 to 20 meters higher, had it been aware of Andotten

Norwegian report on Vassiliev's plane recovery

The Norwegians confirmed all six on board were Russians: Nikolai Romanov, Ivan Miostsepan, Anatoliy Skvortsov, Nikolai Kuznetsov, K. Tjitkan, and Viktor Vassiliev.

Their report also stated, "The site was littered with American currency and American luxury items including nylon stockings, men's and women's clothing, and empty chocolate bar wrappers."

To the best of this author's knowledge, the original conclusion of the Soviet Naval High Command, i.e., missing in action, has never been changed despite the Norwegian findings.

Final Note

Before leaving from the RAF base in Gander, Newfoundland, Vassiliev wrote a handwritten note to thank Chernack and his staff for all they had done to make the first phase of Project Zebra such a success. He mentioned he looked forward to his return to Elizabeth City to work closely on the training and shipment of the other 125+ aircraft. Ironically, the note found its way to Commander Chernack a few short days after Vassiliev and his plane were declared missing in action. Chernack kept that note for almost 40 years before showing it in the 1980s to his son Peter.

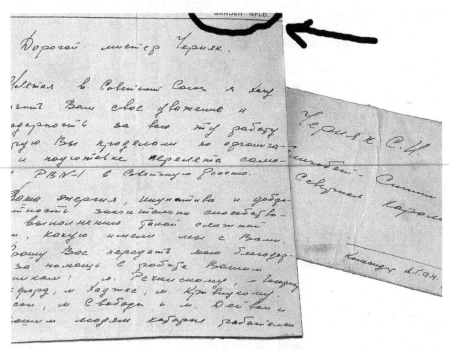

The last note ever written by Colonel Vassiliev

Chapter 12

Soviet Chief No. 2

Col. Maxim Chibisov, more like Chernack than Vassiliev

When it became clear that Vassiliev would not be returning, a new Project Zebra Soviet Commander was needed: a highly-qualified pilot with an excellent knowledge of machinery and extensive experience flying over water. A record review by the staff of Naval Aviation Commander Semyon Zhavoronkov suggested there was a candidate who stood above the others. All that remained was to tell Chibisov of his new mission.

Impeccable Credentials
During his seven-year career, Chibisov had already logged 1,631 hours of seaplane flight time, and had flown 1,475 hours

during the day, another 102 hours at night, and 55 hours under blind conditions. His unit, the 117th regiment, former home of Viktor Vassiliev, had been recognized as the Navy's best boat-based aviation unit for two years in a row.

Chibisov, a respected Soviet Naval Air Commander
before, during, and after Zebra

Chibisov's reputation continued to grow as an experienced commander who had a demonstrated ability to rapidly and efficiently build new air combat units from scratch.

He took pride in a neat, clean appearance, and exhibited amazing endurance and self-confidence. His air and ground decisions were always measured, never casual. Privately, after Barbarossa, he was always concerned about his patriotic young pilots being poorly trained and sent to battle flying old-fashioned planes, which had little chance of victory against the formidable German opponent.

Chibisov was considered the personification of a clear-headed naval officer and pilot. His official personnel file described him as "Strong-willed, energetic commander who works every day to enhance his overall and tactical level. He is demanding of himself and his subordinates. Concise in his instructions and their monitoring. Politically competent. Soundly assesses the situation and reacts properly. Tries to apply his knowledge to practice under the conditions of war. Rank and position are entirely consistent." [23]

Leaving Family

In early July, Chibisov was summoned to Fleet Headquarters in Vladivostok. There, he learned he was going to head an unnamed special mission.

Chibisov, wife Rosochka, daughter Emma, at Moscow home

"When?" asked wife Rosochka.

"The day after tomorrow," he replied. Chibisov hugged his family goodbye, had one last picture taken with them, and took off, with no real knowledge of what the mission was or when he might return.

In Moscow, he learned he had been appointed the head of the top-secret Project Zebra in America. It was during these meetings that he learned for the first time where his former second in command had been assigned, and how he perished.

---

[23] Across Continents and Oceans, R & C Dynamics, 2011

Despite the secrecy surrounding military missions, some vague information about the death of the leader of a top-secret mission leaked out. Rosochka Chibisov learned of the rumor that a Pacific Fleet pilot — a major or a colonel — had been killed. Rosochka became frantic and secured an appointment with the Pacific Air Fleet Commander. He told her that "You will not be hearing from Maxim for some time, but I swear he is safe and sound."

Coming to America

Chibisov had never traveled internationally, but now he — along with a group of pilots and specialists — was sent to America via the Southern Route in order to get a closer look at the Nomads' most traveled route to the Black Sea. As he traveled over and through Egypt, Libya, and Morocco, the fastidious Chibisov made some observations in his diaries: "The architecture of the Eastern Cities is fantastically beautiful, but the streets are full of dirty workers in torn clothes, and there are many beggars."[24]

In Morocco, he noticed an abundance of stores and taverns. Growing up in a Soviet society which believed working hard was the norm, he wondered, "Why are there such a large number of loafers sitting around in cafes and bars?"

He concluded that these casual liberal manners prevailed in all foreign capitalist countries. He even saw that attitude in the behavior of the American pilots during flight. "They frequently put the plane on auto-pilot while they sat around joking, talking, and laughing."

[24] Diaries of Maxim Chibisov

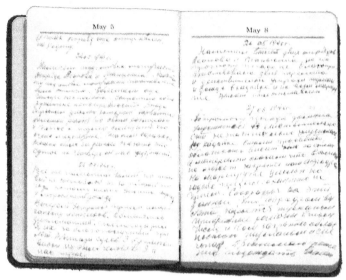

Pages from Chibisov's diary.

Somehow, the pilots learned Chibisov was a Soviet flying ace. While on auto-pilot, the American senior pilot asked if he'd like to take the helm.

His diary recorded the experience. "During the flight to America, I was fortunate enough to fly the advanced Douglas C54 for three and a half hours. It was pleasant and even flattering. I had no problem learning to fly the machine."

As the pilot flew over the wide expanse of the Atlantic, his plane experienced unexpected turbulence in the form of lightning storms and heavy rain squalls. When the plane returned to normal flight, he wrote: "I now better understand the conditions our pilots will most certainly face."

As he entered the continental United States, he immediately realized things were not exactly as he had been led to believe back home. "We are flying over bustling big cities. They appear to be major industrial areas located by the shores of rivers, lakes, and the ocean. There is a lot of green in the cities." Gradually, the landscape became more rural. "The large farms below have a very pleasant appearance. They are situated like small islands surrounded by well-planned fields. Each farmstead includes vast land for farming, and nice highways border the plots."

On August 14, 1944, Maxim Chibisov landed in Elizabeth City. That first night, thinking about his wife and child, he made what we would be the last diary entry for a while. "We arrived safe and sound in Elizabeth City, a small town which appears to have almost no industry, nice architecture, fully paved streets, and more stores than a typical Soviet city many times its size."

According to his notes, he stopped in one shop to purchase some soap, a toothbrush, and other essentials. He also noted "even though no one spoke Russian, the people were all very friendly but spoke an unfamiliar American dialect."

Flight Records

Despite his relaxed demeanor (compared to Vassiliev), Chibisov kept meticulous logbooks. Like Gagarin, he knew these documents might one day be part of history. If one looks closely at his logbooks, one will even find a few R&R flights up the East Coast.

A page from Chibisov's extensive logbook

Chapter 13

New Challenges

Battlefield reports suggested that the Nomads were performing well in the Atlantic Theater. But more planes were needed, and the Northern Route through Alaska would become increasingly treacherous during the winter months due to freezing temperatures, high winds, and icy landing conditions. Chibisov and Chernack had to develop Plan B.

There was also the matter of increasing Japanese aggression. Stalin was now certain of impending war with Japan in the Pacific Theater and he began to secretly prepare his forces. He considered the use of heavily-armed Nomads critical to the destruction of the Japanese Navy's powerful Pacific Fleet.

After consultation with the Royal Air Force, Chibisov and Chernack developed Plan B: the Southern Route.

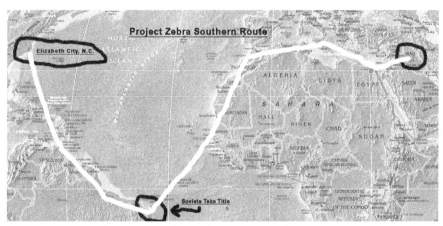

Southern Route ferried approximately 100 Nomads

Unfamiliar South

Like the Northern Staging Route, this Southern Route was not without its challenges. It was completely unfamiliar to Project Zebra pilots, despite the fact it was a German- and Japanese-free route all the way to the Black Sea. Also, the many intermediary refueling stops in South America and Africa required coordination with the British Royal Air Force (RAF), which operated the bases and provided repair crews as necessary.

Fortunately, the RAF also had experience flying the Soviet Nomad's sister plane, the Catalina. While the RAF Catalina did not have the same advanced electronics, bombsites, and ordnance capability, many of the flying principles were the same. And, like the Americans and Soviets, they were so fascinated by these flying boats that they took their own public relations pictures for the folks back home.

RAF crews proudly demonstrate their fondness for the Catalina

The Project Zebra flight plan was to leave Elizabeth City with American pilots and RAF crews, travel south over the Atlantic Ocean, making a series of refueling stops on the way to the RAF operated Belem airbase in Natal, Brazil, just south of the equator. There, Russian crews took possession of the planes and flew them to Morocco, Egypt, and Iran before ultimately landing in Habbaniyah, Iraq. From there, the Russian crews took sole possession and completed the flight to the oil-rich fields of Baku, not far from Odessa, Ukraine. To complete this complicated plan, Chernack worked closely with his RAF counterpart, D.H.C. Fry.

Jovial, professional RAF Commander Fry

One of the things Chernack learned about working with Fry was that he believed strongly in clarity of communication. His frequent reports to Chernack were always concise, often including suggestions made by the British high command for Zebra operating improvements.

SECRET   SECRET

HEADQUARTERS

No. 45 (LANTIC TRANSPORT) GROUP

ROYAL AIR FORCE

TELEPHONE: MONTREAL AIRPORT,
WALNUT 7721   DORVAL, QUEBEC,

TO: Lt. S. I   Chernack
            Officer-in-Charge Project Zebra
            Patrol Plane Base
            Elizabeth City, N. C.

FROM: Officer Commanding
            R.A.F. Transport Command
            Elizabeth City, N. C.

REFER.:   EC/11/AIR

DATE: 10th November, 1944

Sir:

      ~~I have the honour to report that I am commanded by my~~
Headquarters in Montreal to ascertain whether the United States
Navy have any objection to aircraft on the "lightup" movement being
sent from Elizabeth City direct to Trinidad. My Headquarters con-
siders that   ful purpose is being served by stopping at San
Juan.

      I am further   manded that crews should, if possible,
be brief   t Natal to in   e that they arrive at Bathurst in the
morning s   t they   e able to leave Bathurst the same night,
as this has   st practical arrangement.

      I will be grateful, therefore, if you would take steps
to forward this letter to the proper authorities and let me have an
answer on these two matters as soon as it is convenient.

                              ur to be,

                   our obedient Ser

                   D.H.C. Fry, Squadron Lead
                   fficer Commanding

Nov 10, 1944. Fry to Chernack: All is well.

    The first Southern Route test included six Russians, American
Interpreter Nester Holtz, and six RAF officers: Bob Wargent, Seth
Yarrington, Clyde Pangborn, Jock Horan, and Barry Moffit.
Recognizing the historic nature of this new partnership, Moffitt asked
the Belem airbase photographer to record the Russian-RAF presence.

Natal, Brazil. Only known picture of Russian-RAF Zebras

Chapter 14

Chief Ski

Walter Krivitsky was called the Chief for good reason

Over 200 Soviet officers and enlisted men were trained to fly the advanced Nomads by about a dozen American Navy trainers, supported by scores of civilians who — day and night — kept the lights burning, the fuel flowing, and the runway operational.

Walter Krivitsky was arguably one of the most important members of Project Zebra. He was born in Ukraine and, at the age of 20, fled to America during the Bolshevik transition.

Ellis Island

Krivitsky arrived at Ellis Island with only the clothes on his back and a small bag with an additional pair of pants and a shirt. When he reached the desk of the immigration officer, the man asked where he was from. Krivitsky responded "the Ukraine."

The officer asked, "Where is that? Haven't had one of those before."

That was the first-time Krivitsky realized most Americans knew little of the rest of the world. He replied simply, "Ukraine is the Eastern section of the Soviet Union."

The officer nodded. He asked Krivitsky what he planned to do in the United States. Krivitsky shrugged his shoulders; he had no idea. The officer, noticing the heavy accent, assumed Krivitsky might not have understood the question. "Do you have a profession, like carpenter or plumber?" Krivitsky shook his head no. "So, what can you do?" asked the officer.

Krivitsky smiled. "I'm a good sailor." The officer asked if he'd like to serve in the United States Navy. He pointed to a colorful recruitment poster on the wall nearby, "Maybe you should consider the Navy. Use your skills and see the world."

COME ALONG
learn something, see
something in the
U S NAVY
ample shore leave
for inland sights

Recruiting poster that attracted Krivitsky

Krivitsky replied, "Why not?" It turned out to be the right decision; the Navy would become the only job Krivitsky ever had. By the time of Zebra, Krivitsky was a naturalized American citizen who had reached the rank of Chief Petty Officer with five black hash marks, or service stripes, on his dress coat sleeve. (Each service stripe represented four years of service.) Typically, officer service stripes were in gold. One evening after many drinks at the officer's club, Krivitsky explained why his were black instead of gold.

"When I was a seaman, I had been given the boring job of chipping paint off a weathered metal ship section. This guy comes along in a suit and shiny shoes. He sees me working real slow. He asks what I'm doing. I tell him, 'I'm fucking off 'til quittin' time.' The guy asked me my name and left. The next day I discovered two things: the civilian was my Chief Petty Officer, and my personnel file now had a serious reprimand."

Workarounds

During his formative years in the Soviet Union, Krivitsky was forced to do without what Americans considered life's simple basics. Like many immigrants of the time, he learned to survive by becoming a master of workarounds. He quickly learned that America was different. The American military was a place of plenty — but you needed to know what you wanted and how to procure same. Over time, his reputation as the man who could "Getum anything" became well known, and he was affectionately nicknamed Chief Ski.

Despite his ability to tap into American abundance, Ski retained a fierce sense of pride in his Soviet heritage. As the American officers learned, every Soviet citizen was taught from birth to honor and respect the Motherland (*Rodina-mat'*). Ski was no different. Put another way, he was happy with what he had, but he never forgot his roots. When the American officers suggested that what we had in States was better than in the Soviet Union, he would raise his eyebrows and say, "Not true. It was all the same before the war."

At first glance, he had no obvious qualifications for the Zebra mission: he now only spoke a touch of Russian, he couldn't fly or maintain a plane, and he didn't plan or proctor classroom training sessions.

Ice-Cold Cokes

One day, after a particularly long training session in the hot sun, one of the American officers wiped his brow in the shade and mumbled what he would do for a nice cold Coca-Cola.

Gagarin decided to test the Chief's reputation. "Chief, I heard you can pretty much make anything happen."

The Chief saw right through the subtlety. "So, what do you want?"

Gagarin went for the brass ring. "It would be great if we could get one of those red coolers filled with ice and Cokes."

Krivitsky nodded. "We'll see," he replied noncommittally.

Three days later, the officers walked into the headquarters office. There, in the corner, sat a big second-hand red Coca-Cola cooler. Gagarin opened the top. It was filled to the brim with chipped ice and Cokes. Nobody wanted to ask the Chief how he did it. They simply knew that when the ice melted or the Cokes ran down, the cooler would magically be refilled.

Ice cold cokes during and after every training session

The Chief had even managed to override the payment slot so that the Cokes were always free.

Norfolk PX

It was apparent that Chief Ski had an endless source of contacts at the Naval Base in Norfolk, Virginia, which was about an hour's drive from Elizabeth City. Every other Friday, he'd take an empty Navy-issue station wagon and drive to Norfolk, returning the following day with heavily rationed items like five-pound tins of Maxwell House Coffee. We always offered to pay, but Ski would simply reply, "No worries; on the Russian house." Before long, thanks to Ski's largess, the American officers who lived within traveling distance packed a tin or two in their bags for family and friends when they went on weekend leave. "We (the Americans) called the stuff the Chief's Black Market Coffee," said Gagarin.

Maxwell House Coffee. Good to the last drop. Even in 1944.

From time to time, the American officers would sit around Zebra headquarters and talk about the Chief's unusual acquisition skills. They assumed that after 20 years of Naval service, he knew how to barter his way around supply depots. The question was, what did he barter? No American officer — sober or drunk — ever came up with a plausible answer.

Soviet Shopping List

After observing Ski's PX delivery service, Chibisov asked if the Chief would make some purchases for his boys. The Chief obliged. "Just give me your wish list and some money." Gagarin was again called on to explain the term "wish list."

The Soviet Zebra shopping strategy was a highly planned military maneuver. The soldiers knew what they could and couldn't buy in town, so they focused on items they were nonperishable, easily transportable in the Nomad's storage bays, and could command a handsome profit on the Soviet Black Market. The most popular Russian requests were American whiskeys and Camel cigarettes.

Some of the Soviet Zebras most requested PX items

"Before long, every bed and every locker was full, but the inventory kept coming. Made us wonder, where did those boys store all the stuff?" said Gagarin. "We also wondered, but never asked

Chief Ski, if he had included a markup for himself. We figured it was none of our business and he'd just give us his standard 'don't ask' reply."

While Krivitsky was the oil that kept the Zebra personal needs machine running, little was known about his personal life. As Gagarin reminisced years later, "The Navy was his life. He had no children, no kids, no family. I just assume he was probably well-taken care of at one of those old soldiers' homes somewhere."

Chapter 15

Zebra World Headquarters

Project Zebra World Headquarters

At first glance, the exterior of Zebra World Headquarters looked like a standard military issue one-story Quonset hut: a moon-shaped, lightweight, corrugated steel structure, about 20' wide by 49' long and 10' tall at its highest point, and painted in the camouflage brown, yellow and gray. The building had an emergency ladder attached to the side that seemed to go nowhere, and screens on the windows to keep bugs out during the hot, humid summers. Elizabeth City winters were mild, so there was no indoor heating. As Gagarin recalled, "I think I saw a hint of snow twice in two years."

Inside Headquarters

The interior was equally unremarkable: just a large open space dotted with wooden desks, with chairs scattered about. Some desks had a phone, typewriter, or desk fan; others had nothing. In one corner sat Chief Ski's Coca-Cola cooler, in the other a coffeepot that seemed to work around the clock. Since the walls were curved, it was difficult to affix maps, schedules, and other work-related notices. Those items were found in the structure's only room with a window-mounted Carrier air conditioner.

The for-officers-only headquarters facility was shared equally by the Soviets and Americans. Sometimes they grouped in different areas; most time, they did not.

Zebra offices: a modest affair

Occasionally, the Soviets would attempt to speak in English about military matters with their counterparts, without much success. Inevitably, Gagarin would stop what he was doing and go to work at his second job: Zebra's official translator! Gagarin knew from family experience that certain American military slang didn't readily translate into Russian,[25] so he worked with those Soviet officers who were willing to learn a little "conversational American." Before long, the Soviet officers were saying things like "I get cup of java," and "hot, like a nice chilly Coke" in a heavy Russian accent

---

[25] Two frequently used pieces of WW II military slang: Beat your gums" meant stop talking, while "ash cans" was short for submarine depth charges.

Preparing Reports

When the time came to send status reports to superiors, there was no such language confusion — the Americans used Royal brand typewriters while Soviet reports were prepared with a Cyrillic-character typewriter, compliments of the Russian Embassy in Washington, D.C. Before Project Zebra, no American officer had even seen a typewriter with Cyrillic characters. One curious American officer asked he could type a few letters. A few clacks later, he pulled the paper from the roller and stared at it. "How can you understand this stuff?"

Soviet Cyrillic typewriter made in Italy by Olivetti

War Room

The only room with an air conditioner served as the conference room. It was where the Russian officers grieved when they learned of Vassiliev's disappearance, and where they wondered who their next commander would be.

It was here that Maxim Chibisov appeared for the first time in August 1944. Gagarin rose from his chair and saluted out of respect. Chibisov stared at the taller Gagarin, then smiled and stuck out his enormous hand in friendship. That single gesture told every Soviet and American officer in that room that the remainder of the Zebra mission — however long that might be — would be different from the first three months under Vassiliev.

Planning military exercises in the Zebra war room

It was also the room where training plans were developed and war news was discussed. As always, Gagarin would pick up the local paper and describe in Russian what it said, while the Soviets would ask questions. It was during these moments that Chibisov realized Gagarin was the glue that held the mission together.

In time, Gagarin and the others learned Chibisov was culturally inquisitive. He saw Project Zebra as a once-in-a-lifetime opportunity for him and his men to see the real America and learn as much as possible about the American way. Frequently, he would joke, "The more we understand 'the capitalist,' the better for all of us."

No Translation Necessary

The room with the air conditioner was also the one place where both sides could explore the most popular men's magazines of the day — the racier, the better — without the need for translation. The lone dual language utterances centered around, "Ahhh," Whoa," and "Mmmmm."

Popular American and Soviet men's magazines during the War

Initially, the Americans didn't realize there were no such equivalent men's magazines in the Soviet Union. The magazines that did exist were primarily women's fashion magazines, which featured aspirational women in generally conservative dresses.

Stalin's communications strategy was to celebrate the Soviet Union as a modern, progressive society while implying to the general population that unshakeable loyalty to the Motherland would one day be rewarded all with such accouterments.

Improved Telephone Service

As more planes were produced and more Soviet crews trained, the number of phone calls to and from the base to the embassies and the Naval Aircraft Factory increased dramatically. Because Zebra was top secret, all calls were initiated and received at Zebra World Headquarters.

At that time, an oversized brick utility building, which covered most of the block between Cobb and Fearing Streets in downtown Elizabeth City, served as the central offices for the Norfolk & Carolina Telephone Companies. These serviced most of North Carolina and Virginia through massive operator switchboards. At the height of the war, there were more than 70 female switchboard operators.

In December 1944, Gagarin, who oversaw telecommunications, complained to Chernack that the base telephone service had slowed. Chernack said simply, "So fix it."

"How?" asked Gagarin.

Chernack replied, "Use your imagination." Chernack had organized a little Zebra Christmas party at the Officer's Club. He suggested Gagarin spread the word that all off-duty operators were invited to the party. To Gagarin's surprise, and the delight of the men, more than 40 women showed up; they giggled, laughed, and drank the night away.

Christmas party with hosts Chernack and Gagarin,
and the N&C telephone operators

A good time was had by all, including Chernack and Chibisov. The speed of the Zebra telephone service improved noticeably after the party.

Chapter 16

Zebra Bus Company

Downtown shopping, Elizabeth City 1944.

Despite initial language barriers, the Soviet crews loved shopping in Elizabeth City. The wide selection and ready availability of consumer goods were dramatically better than what they were accustomed to in the Motherland. And prices were significantly lower than the black-market prices at home.

Silver Certificates

Shopping American was not without a learning curve. The first group of Soviet shoppers returned to the base frustrated and empty-handed. As they explained to Gagarin, they had gone into a few stores to buy some dresses and underwear for their wives, but the clerk behind the counter refused their American dollars. As an officer explained in Russian, "They say they are not real American dollars."

Gagarin asked to look at their money. The Soviets took several oversized dollar bills out of their pockets, which they had received as pay from the Russian Embassy in Washington.

(Russian officers were paid about 30 percent of what their American counterparts received. Disbursements via the Embassy eliminated awareness of that difference.)

Rare vintage silver certificates nobody wanted

Gagarin looked at the vintage silver certificate. He knew what the problem was immediately: these were pre-World War I bills that were no longer in circulation. They were not unimportant, however; they were worth about ten times the face value as collectors' items.

His solution was simple. He convinced the Soviets the "bills were too old." But he told them not to worry; he thought some American officers collected old coins and currency.

Gagarin gave the Soviets the good news. The collectors would be happy to exchange the "old money" with their "new money" on a dollar-to-dollar basis. The Russians readily agreed.

A few Soviets again went to town the next day with the "new money." They returned with armfuls of American-made goods. This ten to one exchange program continued until the Embassy ran out of silver certificates and switched to current currency…. about six months and thousands of dollars later.

Dry Goods

The Soviets were as organized about shopping as they were in combat. They quickly discovered Elizabeth City was a town of fabric mills. And cotton mills meant women's clothing, women's underwear, women's silk stockings, and bolts of fabric to make clothes — all products that would sell easily back home on the Soviet black market.

Their favorite dry goods store was Robinson's, on Water Street. It was known to have the largest selection and inventory.

Shoppers came from miles around to visit Robinson's Mills

Flora Robinson, 104 years old at the time of the interview, recalled vividly, "Daddy knew when them Russian boys were going home, they would clear the shelves. But he said they were always courteous, and paid in US dollars. They didn't say much. They would point to Daddy's ladder and then point to the shelves. Daddy would nod, then they would make a chain passing bolt after bolt down until the shelves were bare. Colors and patterns didn't mean a thing."

Flora Robinson recalls Soviet soldiers at her daddy's store

"Them boys would pile the goods on the counter and point to a pad and pencil. Daddy would add up the total, write it on a piece of paper, and the men would nod, collect the money between themselves, and pay us."

Initially, the Soviets thought the number written on the pad was a starting point for negotiation, as in the USSR But they quickly learned the price was the price, and it was always cheaper than the prices at the State-run stores back home.

"I remember telling this nice American officer about our sales process," said Flora. "He explained he spoke Russian. He taught Daddy one word. Next time they came in boys piled the stuff on the counter, Daddy held up his pad and said 'skol-ka' (how much). The men smiled and nodded. Skol-ka, skol-ka. Only Russian Daddy ever learned."

Another Soviet Zebra favorite was the F. & W. Woolworth's store on Main Street, because they could buy lots of cheap socks and shoes from the self-service bins without the need for much English. They never concerned themselves about style, size, or color. Whatever the bins contained was good enough.

Sometimes, the men would carry the entire bin to the cashier and say one of the few English words they would learn, "How much?" The clerk would then write the number on a piece of paper, and hand it to whomever appeared to be in charge.

Woolworth on Main Street, where the Soviet Zebra
were introduced to product bins

The men never bought clothes for themselves, but they were very appearance conscious. Chibisov advised his men again and again that a "Soviet officer must look good, especially abroad." Consequently, many of them became regular customers at local shops like H.H. Lavenstein's on Pearl Street for trouser and coat alterations, Bill Williams on Cypress for shoe repairs, and barber Paul Burgess on Walnut for haircuts. For shaving razors, blades, and creams, Chibisov recommended Stephenson's drugs on Main Street. "Best selection at best price," he would tell his men in Russian at the base.

Paul Burgess, who was good friends with Flora Robinson's father, John, would always keep an ear out to determine when the latest Russian crews might be leaving for their home. That way, John would make sure his shelves were full.

Every shopping excursion ended the same way: an ice-cold glass of Coca-Cola and an ice cream cone at The Apothecary Shop. One day, the clerk saw Major Salnikov staring at an unfamiliar sandwich sign. "Y'all want a BLT?"

Salnikov responded, "Da, BLT ya all." Soon, the clerk returned with a triple-decker sandwich stacked with thick slabs of bacon, beefsteak tomatoes, cheese, and lots of mayonnaise. Because of food shortages in his homeland, Salnikov had never seen such a grand sandwich. He devoured every morsel.

One day at the Officer's Club, they were serving sandwiches at lunch time. The serving table was filled with bacon, cheese, and tomatoes, among other items. Salnikov smiled at the mess chef and said, "BLT ya all." The American Zebras couldn't stop laughing at Salnikov's new-found fluency.

Ration Game

Shopkeepers understood the visiting Russians (the town did not call them Soviets) were allies and friends. They always treated them kindly and with respect, particularly after one of the shopkeepers accidentally discovered the Soviets would pay a bit more than the current market price.

The Soviets weren't stupid. They knew all about rationing from the Homeland, so they had no problem paying a bit of a premium to buy extra liquor, cigarettes, and other rationed items than the local townspeople were buying by playing a little game with retailers. When they were ready to pay, the shopkeeper would ask them for their ration stamps. They would play dumb, make believe they didn't understand.

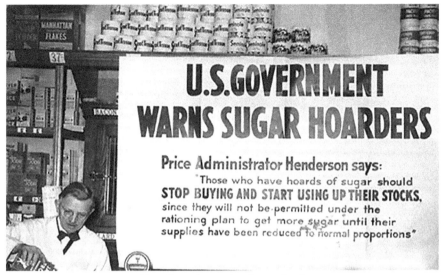

Bending the rationing rules?

They would ask each other what the shopkeeper said in Russian, then shrug their shoulders and put money on the counter. The shopkeeper would play along by making believe he or she was frustrated, then simply say, "Okay." Eventually, all the shopkeepers learned another Russian word: *spaciba* (thank you).

Transport Conundrum

The desire to shop put strains on the base's limited transportation capacity. Initially, Gagarin arranged for one of the American enlisted men to drive a small group to the heart of downtown, and return to the same spot to pick them up two hours later. But the Zebra motor fleet consisted of *one* six-seat Navy issued station wagon, so the frequency of shopping requests was becoming disruptive; there were more requests than one man could handle. Chernack told Chibisov, "Shopping was not a Naval problem or a Project Zebra mandatory."

Chibisov did his research and called the local cab company, Bank's Taxi, which welcomed the new business.

Chibisov's short-lived transportation solution

But taking the cost of the cabs from the enlisted men's pay took a heavy toll on their purchasing power. Chibisov discussed the matter with Chernack, who responded, "Not a Naval problem or a Zebra mandatory."

American Ingenuity

Gagarin told Chibisov not to worry. He had already concluded this was a problem for Chief Ski. After hearing the issue, Ski leaned back in his chair and nodded, "I may have an idea; let me see what I can do."

One day later, the Chief Ski showed up at the headquarters building with an old-school bus that had a current set of Navy plates. As Chibisov and Gagarin walked toward the Chief, he raised his hand and said: "Don't ask."

Chibisov shook his head. "It is so easy to accomplish so much in America. Maybe someday…"

Gagarin's unique perspective of Russian history suggested "someday" was a long way away. The orderly minded Gagarin decided that he and Chibisov should develop a "best practices" plan. A day later, they explained the plan to Chernack, who readily agreed.

The bus would make one trip to town center in the morning and one in the afternoon. There would also be one final pre-dinner pickup.

Chief Ski to the rescue… again

The schedule was posted on the bulletin boards in both the officer and enlisted men's barracks. That way nobody could say they didn't know. Eventually, the process became known as the Zebra Bus Service. No Soviet Zebra ever missed the last pickup; nobody wanted to miss dinner or post-meal libations.

If disputes arose, they were to be settled by Gagarin, now the CEO (Chief Executive Officer) of Zebra Airlines *and* the Zebra Bus Company.

Chapter 17

Three Square Meals+

Circa 1943. Russian shoppers in line for hours to buy bread. Note empty shelves.

The Russian economy during the Stalin years was ruled by a series of Five-Year Plans intended to put the Soviet Union on equal footing with their more developed West European neighbors. The plans contained two major categories: Group A - Heavy Industry, and Group B - Consumer Goods. The first plan, introduced in 1928, focused almost exclusively on Group A. Consequently, consumer need and demand was only partially satisfied.

The second Five-Year Plan, introduced in 1933, was supposed to rebalance the focus to include the production of more consumer goods. At that time, about 60 percent of consumer goods were distributed through state-owned stores and cafeterias accessible to employed workers. [26]

---

[26] Everyday Stalinism: Ordinary Life in Extraordinary Times. Sheila Fitzpatrick. Oxford University Press. 1999. See References.

The system had sporadic success, and the rationing of goods became a fact of everyday life... for most. Despite continued shortages, lines, and rationing, Stalin declared two years later in posters placed all over Russia that "Life has become more joyous." [27]

Stalin's cheerful "Life is More Joyous" propaganda

Despite the obvious systematic shortcomings, the State maintained absolute authority over distribution.

Before long, an abusive haves and have-not's secondary system evolved. There were poorly stocked bureaucratic state and cooperative outlets for 95 percent of Russian citizens, and a well-stocked specialized network of goods and services for the privileged 5 percent.[28] These obvious inequalities led the resourceful Russians to buy and sell goods in the *Shadow Economy*, known in America as the Black Market. During the early 1930s, despite the implementation of Stalin's heralded Five-Year Economic Plans, the masses experienced extreme famine and shortage. People sold family items simply to buy the basics needed to survive.

---

[27] Soviet Poster Collection. Wright Museum of Art.

[28] Colored Markets in the Soviet Union. See References.

Soviet Soldiers

Frontline Soviet troops fared no better than ordinary citizens. Even though Soviet soldiers were considered a rationing priority, they were only allotted 3,000 to 3,500 calories a day, which was 60 to 100 percent less than British and German combat troops received. A typical frontline meal consisted of Kasha — a buckwheat porridge; Okroshka — a cold soup of raw vegetables; boiled potatoes; and Tyurya —a cold broth with bread soaked in a fermented beverage. [29] Meat was almost nonexistent in Red Army field kitchens, which recalls another sadly, humorous "Soviet Story of War.".

An American cargo ship shuttling Lend-Lease supplies hit turbulent waters near the northern port of Murmansk. To ensure delivery, the Americans opened the large iron doors of their cargo ship so the smaller Soviet vessel could enter. The Soviets saw sacks of flour and piles of canned Spam. Their eyes bulged in anticipation. One sailor stepped up with a big can of Spam, opened the lid, cut the Spam into small pieces and hollered: "OK, comrades, go ahead: Help yourselves."

The Soviets hesitated, unsure what the hollering meant. No one spoke a word of the other's language. The young American sailor smiled, put a piece of Spam in his mouth and gestured for the Russians to do the same. The soldiers attacked the open cans, then cried as they ate. [30]

Against these harsh realities, the Soviet Zebras knew how fortunate they were to have well-balanced meals three times a day, every day.

Breakfast

The officers and enlisted men had a typical, sit-down, full American breakfast: cereal and fruit, eggs and bacon or sausage, toast, coffee, and juice. Initially, the Soviets sat at tables by themselves, not

---

[29] Soviet Stories of War. See References.

[30] Soviet Stories of War. See References.

because they were unsociable but because they didn't speak a word of English. On numerous occasions, Gagarin, because of his fluency, would invite himself to sit with the Soviets. He was always welcomed with a smile and a "da."

From time to time, questions arose that exposed cultural differences.

Salnikov: "Why do we eat off plates, while our men eat off metal pans?"

Chernack: "Because we're officers."

Salnikov: "Oh." (There was no such distinction in the Soviet military).

Salnikov: "What do seconds mean?"

Chernack: "If you're hungry, eat as much as you want."

The Soviet officers were also confused by certain breakfast cereals like Kellogg's Rice Krispies. They had no idea why cereal had to "Snap, Crackle, and Pop." They also had no idea what puffed rice was or why you puffed something so small.

Some capitalist consumer goods had no Soviet equivalent

The popular cereal staple Cheerios caused confusion. "What did a masked American Cowboy [Lone Ranger endorsement] have to do with a bowl of cereal?"

Lunch

After breakfast, the men broke into flight and ground training groups. Ground training crew lunch took place in the officer's mess hall and usually was comprised of sandwiches made with a variety of meats (turkey, beef, chicken, and ham) and cheeses (American, Swiss, and cheddar).

One day, one of the American Zebras, Lt. Mohler, saw Soviet Zebra Captain Tetdoev was enjoying a stack of sandwiches he had made at the self-serve counter. Mohler tried to make conversation, "Taste good?"

The Soviet officer nodded, "Da, meat."

Mohler looked at the sandwich stack. "So, what did you put in it?"

Tetdoev: "Meat."

The American assumed his counterpart misunderstood. "I meant, what kind of meat is in the sandwich?"

Tetdoev stared and shrugged. "Meat." Soviet State stores never differentiated between types of meat when it was available; meat was meat.

Teams involved in flight training usually landed the plane on the Sound and ate lunch onboard. The Nomads each had a small kitchen and refrigerator, so they made coffee, ate pre-prepared sandwiches, and enjoyed some fresh fruit. On sunny days, the crews dined al fresco by taking life preservers outside and sitting on the mammoth lower wing.

Soviet and American Zebras prepare for lunch break

Breaks

Afternoon breaks were unknown among USSR workers at the time. But the Zebra team understood the idea quickly. Occasionally, they would walk over to the little café on base and have doughnuts and coffee. But most afternoons they just hung out at "World" headquarters. The chairs were comfortable, the cookies tasty, the coffee plentiful, and the men's magazine library extensive. One afternoon, Chibisov, who knew coffee was carefully rationed in the States and Russia, asked "Why does Project Zebra always have coffee?"

Two Americans responded in unison, "Chief Ski." Chibisov committed their answer to memory.

Dinner

Dinner was always more relaxed: the day was over, and the Soviets knew whatever they ate would be both an improvement over a Soviet meal and a surprise. But, as with some of the training terms, there were dinner entrees that did not translate. "Explaining what corned beef hash was to a Russian was hysterical," recalled Gagarin. Each meal always had multiple components — protein, vegetable, fruit, starch, and dessert.

"Whether you were talking about the officers or the enlisted seamen, those guys never missed a meal, and never left a morsel on their dishes or trays," recalled Gagarin.

Nightcaps

The high point on most days was the after-dinner nightcaps and relaxed, candid conversation at the Officers Club.

The American officers learned the Soviet soldier's daily wartime alcohol allotment was a meager 100-150 grams (about 1 ½ shots) of barely drinkable vodka. The Club had no limits; drinks were cheap and the availability of brands was enormous by Soviet standards. Commander Chibisov was content to let the men enjoy the camaraderie so long as there was no excessive drinking or embarrassing behavior. He wanted his American counterparts to remember their Soviet partners as disciplined, professional, patriotic, and determined. The most frequently requested drink was scotch, and the favorite Soviet brand was Johnnie Walker.

The Soviet Zebras' preferred brand of Scotch

When the Soviets were asked why Johnnie Walker, a Soviet officer held up a magazine "First Choice" advertisement with Johnnie Walker strutting past a collection of country club patrons. "Most American," he said. Nobody ever asked why.

Candid Conversations

The Americans quickly learned that the discussion of political matters was taboo, and so they obliged their guests, not knowing if the silence was a direct order or just natural reticence to discuss political matters.

As time passed, the Soviets began to observe firsthand that some of what they had been told about America and Americans was not quite true. They saw America's patriotic fervor, its warmth and generosity, and its effacing sense of humor. But their immersion in the Communist way was deeply ingrained.

Every so often, the conversation went from social to candid. The merits of Soviet socialism versus American capitalism were debated late into the evening.

Who won? "Nobody and everybody," reminisced Gagarin. "We realized Americans and Soviets are more alike than different, despite all the 'us and them' political rhetoric and propaganda.

"We agreed the world would be a better place if we celebrated each other's culture's differences, rather than harboring mutual suspicions.

"And, not least importantly, we were forever bound by our Project Zebra partnership. A mission that we knew would add a unique page to history and be a part of our legacies to our families, our friends, and our countries."

Chapter 18

Play Time!

Captain Tetdoev gets ready to race

The Elizabeth City base covered about four square miles and included the Coast Guard Station, an air traffic control tower, two runways, and several buildings dedicated to general Navy operations, in addition to Project Zebra.

Scooter Races

Five days a week, the Project Zebra team would deliver new flight plans to air traffic control, about a half mile from the Zebra headquarters hut. At first, they walked back and forth. To improve efficiency, Chernack procured three Navy gas-powered scooters. Since there was no such vehicle in the Soviet Union at the time, it took several weeks for Chibisov's team to get the hang of it. Once they did, they zoomed around like a bunch of exited kids.

Before long, the Soviets decided to race each other during free time for packs of American cigarettes, with free time being mostly in the evening before sunset. There were about a dozen regulars. They mapped out a course that avoided the runways, and both Chibisov and Chernack. One day, two of the racing drivers came within inches of bumping into each other as they headed for the finish line. Nearby, Gagarin shook his head, "Your boys ought to be a bit more careful. You heard what Vassiliev did to the officer smoking in bed."

Homemade Speedboats

The left side of the Elizabeth City base was Navy and the other side Coast Guard. One Saturday, some Soviet enlisted men were eating sandwiches while watching the locals race up and down the Pasquotank River. The Soviets were soon joined by some of the American enlisted men.

Somehow, they figured out how to communicate. Both parties agreed to race on the river in *Coast Guard-issue speedboats.* (The Soviets had no idea there was no such boat). They would drag-race about a quarter of a mile up the river from the Water Street Harbor. The winner would receive free drinks from the losers until he couldn't drink anymore.

That week, the Coast Guard maintenance crew cleverly took four aircraft pontoons and strapped outboard motors to the rear with a little makeshift seat. Two of the boats had the Red Army star, and two had the US Navy blue seal on their bow.

Russians and American race on the Pasquotank

When they arrived at the harbor the day of the races, there were about 50 to 100 observers. Minutes later, the boats were zooming down the river. A Russian sergeant, Oleg Sapunov, won by several lengths. That evening, Sgt. Sapunov drank until he passed out.

Chess and Backgammon

Most evenings after dinner, Chibisov, Gagarin, and a few other Soviet, British, and American officers would have a few nightcaps, listen to the Tommy Dorsey and Benny Goodman bands, and sing along with Meg Whitman and Vera Lynn.

Chibisov observed a few Americans playing backgammon. Gagarin explained the rules. "Like chess, but different," smiled Chibisov.

Gagarin asked if they would like to learn to play. "Like on-the-job training," said Chibisov. After a few practice rounds, which the Americans won handily, they played for real. During the next two evenings, the Soviets didn't come close to winning.

Chibisov waved his men over. They huddled and spoke quietly, and nodded their heads. Chibisov spoke for the group. "You Americans kind enough to teach backgammon, we return the favor in chess."

The Americans laughed confidently, "We're also pretty good at chess."

British teach Soviets backgammon as Americans watch

"Not just chess. Soviet chess."

It was now closing time. "Tomorrow night, okay?" asked Chibisov.

The Soviets, who had been taught to play chess since childhood, knew that patience and planning multiple moves made up *the long game* path to victory over an opponent. Chibisov realized these traditional strategies were not the American way. Winning at chess was the way to free drinks. Privately, he told his officers "Play for drinks. Your glass will always be full."

Gagarin, a Magna Laude from MIT, volunteered to play the first round the next evening. "The Russians knew what I was going to do before I did it. I think the game lasted ten minutes." A determined Gagarin insisted on a rematch. The results were the same, only a minute or two faster.

According to unofficial anecdotes, after being embarrassed again and again, the American Zebras threw in the towel. The Russians liked the idea of *guaranteed* free drinks. Chibisov proposed a change in strategy. "Let them win once in a while." [31]

---

[31] Diaries and notes of Gagarin. See References.

Slaviansky's Concert

There is only one thing Russians love more than chess: classical music. At the time of Zebra, a passionate but aging Slavic diva, Madame Margarita Agreneva-Slaviansky, tried to secure government funding for the Slaviansky Russian Trio,[32] a traveling musical group that would celebrate the Slavic culture in song and dance to boost wartime morale. Despite her famous father and his connections among the Soviet privileged, she was unable to obtain investors. She moved to America and ultimately obtained funding from Hollywood producer Edgar Ulmer, a Ukrainian known for making good films on small budgets.

From 1942 to 1945, the trio performed popular Slavic war songs and Balkan folk-dances at small towns and cities around the United States. On Thursday evening, June 29, 1944, the trio appeared at the State Teachers College in Elizabeth City.

Flamboyant Princess Slaviansky and her Royal Company

---

[32] Orest Martynowych. The Showman and the Ukrainian Cause. See References.

Chernack heard about the performance from the mayor, who suggested, "Those Russian boys you've got there might like to see the show." Chibisov agreed. Chief Ski agreed to drive the Zebra bus. About 20 Russians attended the performance, although only Chibisov and Chief Ski spoke any English.

About halfway through the show, Madame Slaviansky sang her father's most famous composition, *Volga Boatman*. Tears rolled down the cheeks of most Zebras. "One day soon, we hear our music at home," said Chibisov emotionally. Towards the end of the performance, Slaviansky introduced the soldiers to the audience, who applauded. The men waved in appreciation.

They then returned to base in the bus and headed for the Officer's Club. The next morning, Chibisov told Chernack that his men were genuinely surprised that someone in America knew something about Russia. "First time," he said.

A story appeared in the Daily Advance Newspaper the following evening: "Russians Here Given Trip Home at Concert."

Daily Advance story about the concert and its Russian audience

Chapter 19

Night at the Movies

The cinematic contributions of Lyubov Orlova
were finally recognized in 2001

One evening a week was movie night in the Elizabeth City Naval Base gymnasium.

The enlisted men would unfold 300+ chairs and arrange them in neat rows of 10. A six-foot square screen would be opened and braced against the front wall. At the other end of the room sat a 35 MM projector with a wire taped to the floor so that speakers could be placed to the left and right of the screen.

It didn't take long for the Americans to realize that the Soviets loved brassy American musicals, and so that became the dominant genre. The general assumption was that musicals required less language fluency than dramas and comedies. While partially true, there were other important reasons for this preference — extravagant

Western-style musicals and their drop dead sexy, leggy actresses simply did not exist in the Soviet cinema.

Soviet Movies

In the early 1930s, Stalin decided the Communist party should exercise complete control over artistic cinema expression. So, he created Soyuzkino (pronounced Sa-yus-kin-a). The agency reviewed every screenplay, approved all production plans, made mandatory edits or revisions, and monitored the distribution of finished films. Movies also followed a uniform style known as *Socialist Realism.* Films had to have simple, broad-appeal storylines; positive heroes as role models; lessons in good citizenship; and support for the then current Communist Party policies. And to eliminate citizen exposure to decadent American capitalist ideology, he banned all foreign films. Not surprisingly, the quantity and quality of filmmaking plummeted during the Stalin years. By 1934, only 45 films had been made, none of which has had enduring creative merit. [33]

American Movies

In contrast, Hollywood executives saw the role of movies much differently than Stalin did. Movies were not for reinforcing political ideology; they were an opportunity to step away from the aftermath of the Great Depression and just feel good. And as the emergence of Hitler darkened the world, Hollywood swept into high gear, perfecting the art of extravagant musicals featuring glamorous female sirens like Betty Grable, Rita Hayworth, and Lana Turner. President Roosevelt was also a great supporter of the entertainment industry. He correctly realized that upbeat movies could have a positive impact on the morale of the American people and American serviceman. [34]

---

[33] The Cinema of Stalinism 1930-1941. See References.

[34] Hollywood Movie Memories. See References.

Soviet Movie Stars

The only genre that seemed to avoid Stalin's heavy hand was musical comedy, assuming they had some reference to contemporary affairs. One Russian man and wife team did better than any other Soviet citizens of the day: Director Grigori Aleksandrov and his actress wife, Lyubov Orlova, who respectively had a brilliant comedic sense and the voice of a nightclub chanteuse, steeped in Soviet modesty, i.e., no bare anything.

Orlova plays the trumpet, jokes, and dances in the Jolly Fellows

Orlova starred in 20 musical comedies, all of which were huge box office hits. The power couple was as if director Steven Spielberg and actress Meryl Streep had combined forces.

Orlova's films never appeared in America, and she was never nominated for an Academy Award. But in 2001, 26 years after she and he husband died two months apart, the New Russian Federation recognized her societal contributions by issuing the stamp at the beginning of this chapter. Today, it is considered a collector's item in Russia.[35]

---

[35] Russiapedia. Prominent Russians: Lyubov Orlova. See References.

American Movie Stars

In Stalin's view, American female movie stars were reminders of capitalistic decadence, which was a clear and present danger to the soul of Russian women. He saw Russian women according to patriarchal traditions: modest and friendly; romantics who loved flowers and poetry; and proud of family values and conventional behavior. Stalin wanted them depicted as such in whatever cinema was available.

Stalin understood that America, in particular, saw Russia as an entirely chauvinistic society. Ironically, Stalin had great respect for the Russian woman's fierce determination to overcome adversity. As history proved, these traits made Russian women reliable combat partners during World War II: flying fighter planes, commanding tank battalions, and running sniper squads along the front lines. In fact, it is estimated that 800,000 Russian women participated in active combat during WWII, which is more than all women of the world before and since. [36]

Initially, the Soviets were reluctant attendees at the weekly Night at the Movies. They had never seen an American movie. They also wondered if their attendance would make its way into a Salnikov or Tiertsiev report to Soviet counter-intelligence. Apparently Chibisov reached some agreement, and the men filled the gym. While the men enjoyed the musical numbers, they also drooled over the sexy antics of Lana Turner, Rita Hayworth, Betty Grable, and others. Chibisov and Gagarin to always sat next to each other in case the Commander needed some additional explanation, which he never did. Both men just liked the companionship, and were on the way to becoming life-long friends.

---

[36] Women in War. See References.

Soviet Zebras liked Lyubov Orlova, but they loved
Lana Turner (l) and Rita Hayworth (r)

Stalin's Chapayev

One evening after the others had left the gymnasium, Chibisov pulled a can of film from a canvas bag he usually carried around with papers and such. "*Chapayev*, want to see? Stalin's favorite.[37] Very popular in the Soviet Union. If you like it, we can show the others." Gagarin looked at his watch. It was almost 9:00 P.M.; he wanted a drink or two before the Officer's Club closed. At the same time, he didn't want to insult his new friend. He offered a compromise, "Colonel, how about we watch some tonight and have a drink?"

---

[37] According to Pravda, the entire country watched Chapayev. See References.

Stalin's favorite movie. Dull, boring, dreadful

The Colonel proudly spooled the film, then pressed the start button. Rather quickly, Gagarin discovered *Chapayev* was a dull, preachy film about a man who leads the peasants and workers in a struggle for the power to contribute to the construction of the idealized Soviet State. Fifteen minutes into the movie, Gagarin waved, "No more." Chibisov never again brought up viewing a Soviet movie.

Lana, Betty, and the Boys

Chibisov came to love the American movies. One a week was simply not enough. On one of his trips to town, he had noticed a few theaters, so one evening he and a few of his senior officers took a cab to town, hoping to see a Betty Grable or Lana Turner musical. Since they couldn't read the marquee at the Carolina Theater on Main Street, they just bought tickets and entered.

Movies in town cause an unexpected problem

They were surprised by two things. The fabric covered seats were incredibly comfortable by all Soviet standards. The movie was a drama starring Greer Garson and without Gagarin, they couldn't understand the words, but the visuals gave them the general idea of the plot. When they returned to the base, Chibisov told Gagarin, "No more American movies without my movie man."

Chapter 20

Skinny Dipping

Soviets and Americans go sightseeing along the beach

The forecast for Saturday, April 21, 1945, was around 75 degrees, about normal for Elizabeth City at that time of year.

Two of the American trainers, Lieutenants Jim Gram and Sid Kellick, drank cold Cokes outside the Zebra Headquarters hut. Gram looked at the clear blue sky. "Wonder if our Soviet friends would like to see the Outer Banks?"

Gagarin broached the subject with Chibisov in Russian, who responded, "Why not?"

Sand Dunes

An hour later, eight soldiers in casual greens were riding in a Navy station wagon, on their way to the beach. After traveling 40 miles west on a four-lane blacktop road, they crossed the tiny bridge at Point Harbor, then turned left onto the narrow two-lane Route 12. The sign read "Welcome to Dare County. 1903 Birthplace of Aviation." Kellick pointed to the historic sign. The Soviets stared blankly. Kellick couldn't speak Russian, and the soldiers couldn't read English. They passed Kitty Hawk park and monument. Gagarin pointed and read the sign: "Kitty Hawk." He didn't realize all Soviets were familiar with the names of Orville and Wilbur Wright, but knew nothing of the phrase Kitty Hawk.

As they entered the village of Nag's Head, Gagarin pointed at the sign and said in Russian, "Welcome to the beach town of Nag's Head. In the summer, people come from all over America to visit."

"Ahhh," said one of the Soviets, "Like Sochi[38] on the Black Sea."

"Not exactly," said Gagarin, who knew. "Same, but warmer." The average temperature in Sochi in April was about 60 degrees, and the water about ten degrees cooler. By contrast, the average Nag's temperature was in the high seventies, with the water in the high sixties.

Suddenly, the tall, powdery-white sand dunes of Jockey Ridge sat to their right. The seagrass waved gently in the breeze. The Soviets became animated, waving and pointing. They had never seen a sand dune in person, much less the tallest active dune system in the Eastern United States. "Like Sahara."

The sand dunes at Jockey Ridge State Park

---

[38] Russia's favorite beach, where the beaches are narrow and covered with small round stones.

Gagarin laughed. "Sahara with water." The men got out of the car and started to walk up the dune. The Soviets took their shoes off and walked in the sand in their bare feet. Two or three of them playfully began to kick the sand on the wide, powdery, deserted beach that was set against foamy waves that stretched as far as they could see.

The men walked down to the glistening water. One of them rolled up his sleeves, swished the water, and said, in Russian, "Like bathwater." Almost immediately the Russians stripped naked, ran into the water, and began to swim like dolphins.

"Jesus, aren't those guys cold?" asked one officer.

"Cold?' said Gagarin. "Have you ever tried to swim in the Black Sea, or worse still, Lake Baikal?"[39]

Soviets enjoy a sunny spring day in the Atlantic Ocean

Fortunately, school was still in session, so no one noticed the butt-naked men laughing and frolicking like children.

No Towels

Not far away, the Coast Guard was performing some rescue maneuvers on the beach. The men heard the shouting in the water. The Coast Guard captain noticed the men were naked. He stormed over and growled at Gagarin. "Soldier, what do you guys think you're

---

[39] Lake Baikal is the largest fresh water lake in the world. It is almost 300 miles long, and contains 40 percent of all the fresh water fish species in the world.

doing! You know this is a public beach; you just can't run around naked." He looked down at the pile of unfamiliar uniforms. "Who the hell are these guys?"

Gagarin responded, "It's a long story."

"I don't want to hear it. If they're crazy enough to want to swim in that damn cold water, just get 'em in their skivvies (underwear)."

Coast Guard practices rescue maneuvers at Nag's Head in the Outer Banks

Gagarin waved the men to shore and explained the situation, as they stood there naked. The men didn't understand what the problem was. All Gagarin could say was, "We don't do things like that here." in Russian. They nodded compliantly, put on their skivvies, and returned to the water.

When they finished swimming, they started running up and down the bright, sunny beach singing in Russian. Gagarin waved for them to stop. They explained that since they didn't have any towels, they were just air drying so their uniforms wouldn't get wet.

Sold Out

The skinny-dipping story made the rounds on base. Chibisov apologized for not understanding. A few days later, Gagarin stopped by Chesson's Department Store to pick up a little something for his mom. The usually well-stocked store seemed depleted. He couldn't help but overhear two clerks talking near an empty merchandise counter with a sign that said, "Men's Swimwear."

"Nice display," laughed the first.

Chesson's was once an Elizabeth City shopping landmark

"Never seen anything like it," said the other. "Those Russian boys came in here the other day and bought every pair of trunks we had in stock."

The other clerk turned and pointed at the empty shelf behind him. "Yup," said the first. "They took all the beach towels, too."

Fish Story

As the summer wore on, it became clear that swimming was a favorite Soviet activity, so Chibisov and his car were quite busy traveling to and from the beach. One day Chibisov, who decided not to join the men, took a walk on the beach. He saw a fisherman in a pair of long rubber leggings pole casting at the ocean's edge. Behind the man was a basket with a few fish sticking out. Chibisov, an avid fisherman, stared. He had never seen a flounder.

"Running real good this morning," smiled the man. Chibisov tried to acknowledge the man with some awkward body language. The man then noticed that Chibisov was wearing a white military jacket and a cap with the Red Star. "You must be one of those Russian boys."

"Da," nodded Chibisov, "Russkie."

Chibisov makes a new friend by the Atlantic Ocean

The man picked up a second pole, pointed to the water, and said, "Want to join me?"

Chibisov got the drift. "Da."

Minutes later, the man had Chibisov in a spare pair of leggings, casting from the shore. Chibisov got a bite, slowly reeled in his catch, and proudly put the flounder in the man's basket. They shook hands, then went back to work. [40] About the same time, one of the skinny dippers had dressed and saw the men; he grabbed his camera and took a picture of his colonel and the man.

---

[40] Diaries of Maxim Chibisov. See References.

Chapter 21

Chibisov's Car

A pleasant surprise arrives at Zebra World Headquarters

The Zebra Bus Company worked well for the enlisted men, but not for the Soviet officers.

The impromptu trip to Nag's Head and the opportunity to skinny dip in the Atlantic Ocean led the men to believe there were many other local sights to see and places to visit. Quietly, they held an all-Soviet officer meeting with Chibisov where they complained about "being tied to the convenience of the American officers, and that the foreigners always got the priority." Chibisov realized his men's complaints could become a distraction to the Zebra mission if not quickly addressed.

Chernack and Chibisov met privately in the Officer's Club, with their translator Gagarin in attendance. Chernack listened respectfully but was very clear. "Maxim, this is not my problem. We've got one Navy station wagon, and nobody is going to issue another."

It's a Chevy!

A few days later, some American officers were having a smoke outside the headquarters hut when a faded black Chevy station wagon pulled up. The heavyset driver, dressed in a Soviet uniform, got out and said, "Colonel Chibisov."

Lt. Jack Gilchrist slid his sunglasses down his nose and asked, "Who are you and why do you want the colonel?"

The blank expression on the man's face said it all. He entire English vocabulary consisted of "Colonel Chibisov." Gagarin was summoned.

Driver Captain Anatoly Gogin arrives from Washington

"Captain Anatoly Gogin has been dispatched from the Soviet Embassy in D.C. Apparently, the car has been issued to Colonel Chibisov to use as he sees fit, and the Captain has been assigned as his driver."

Over the next few days, things changed. Some of the Russian officers began to use the car for trips to town instead of the Zebra Bus Service. Chernack questioned whether they should travel by themselves. Salnikov made it clear his officers had learned how to enter town "without the need for babysitters."

Chibisov was more gracious to Chernack. He explained that with the car, he and his fellow officers could explore the beautiful rural countryside, take a trip to Washington to visit the Embassy, or see some of the "distinctly" American sites like the Washington Monument and the White House. But he had first priority: Chibisov wanted to visit the Kitty Hawk Memorial. He explained that every Soviet child had learned about Orville and Wilbur Wright. Their exploits had first piqued Chibisov's interest in flying. "For me, will be a trip of a lifetime, because unlikely I will ever return after the war."

Driving Papers

At 1000 hours the next morning, Captain Gogin and the Chevy were idling in front of headquarters. Gagarin asked Gogin in Russian if he had an American driver's license. "What for?" responded Gogin. "I drive in Moscow all the time."

Gagarin patiently explained the rules of the road were different in America: you needed to complete a written exam, take a driver's test, and get official papers. The man responded, "No test. Just pay like in Moscow. Get papers." Gagarin tried to explain that he couldn't just bribe people to get "driving papers."

Chibisov approached the men. Gagarin explained the problem. He reinforced his point by explaining that if the man was stopped and didn't have a valid American driver's license, the police could impound the car and leave them both stranded. Chibisov, also unfamiliar with the American motor vehicle process, responded, "Mr. Gagarin, I would be pleased if you could teach him and help him get the papers."

Traffic Test

Gagarin decided to keep Lesson One simple and in Russian. They pulled away from the curb and headed toward town. They came to a slight fork in the road with a sign that read "keep to the right." Anatoly drove straight down the wrong side of the street. Fortunately, there were only two honking oncoming cars. Gagarin sternly instructed him to pull to the side of the road. After explaining the mistake, Anatoly backed up carefully, and they continued on their way.

Typical American road signs circa 1943

They were now on the main shopping street, called, appropriately enough, Main Street. Gagarin explained they would practice parking. Anatoly spotted a fire hydrant and, not realizing it's illegal to park in front of a hydrant, pulled into the space, engine first. Gagarin explained the mistake. Anatoly again said there were no such rules in Moscow and began to back out of the illegal space. It took Anatoly about three tries to park in a legal space.

About a week later, Gagarin felt Anatoly was ready to take a driving test. They went to the police station. The desk officer explained that the examiner who administers the test for the state just left, and they didn't expect him back for a month. He suggested Oleg put his name on the list.

Gagarin tried to be discrete. He explained Oleg was the driver for a foreign officer who needed to travel back and forth to Washington, D.C. The officer looked at Oleg's unfamiliar uniform. "You vouch for him?"

"How about if you just issue a temporary driver's license, and I'll explain the rules of the road?"

"Ain't got no licenses here, sir."

"There's got to be a solution," said Gagarin. "We've got to make our friends happy."

"Tell you what," said the officer. "We'll just keep an eye out for him. Any problems, we'll get to you on the base."

Gagarin shook hands with the policeman and explained the situation to Oleg in Russian. Oleg smiled, nodded, and stuck his hand out. The policeman laughed. "First time I ever shook hands with a Russian. Wait 'til the boys 'round here hear about it. Now you boys take care, and bomb the shit out of that Hitler guy."

Max's License

A few days later, Chibisov was called to a meeting at the Russian Embassy. Gagarin suggested Chibisov take the train, and that he (Gagarin) would personally drive him to Norfolk.

Chibisov responded with pride, "Oleg knows your rules. We're fine." Gagarin tried to explain it was one thing to get pulled over in a small-town like Elizabeth City, where one can always explain things. But Washington, D.C., was another matter.

Maxim proudly removed his Navy ID Card from his wallet. "We are allies. Use my papers as a license, that will do. Can explain working on a special mission at the base."

UNITED STATES NAVY
Identification Card

Maxin N. CHIBISOV
Name

Signature

Color Hair..Brown.. Eyes..Brown..
Weight..199.... Birth..28/7/06..

U.S.S.R.   Void after..7/31/45....

N. Nav. 546   Validating Officer

Soviet Commander Chibisov's US Navy Identification Card

Gagarin imagined a comedic scene in which Oleg is pulled over by a highway patrolman on the Washington Beltway for violating a traffic sign, and Chibisov tries to explain in his deep Slavic accent that they are two Russian guys on a "special mission."

Chapter 22

Wilbur & Orville

The brothers every Russian wanted to meet

Soviet achievements in aviation had been touted as early as the 1920s, and Stalin's strong interest appears to date from 1933. Stalin realized the day would quickly come when military use of planes would grow in importance, and his country needed to be ready.

He also wanted his countrymen — and the rest of the developed world — to believe that the USSR would be a major player in this new arena.

As history books suggest, Stalin had a keen ability to understand and motivate the masses. The first of many propaganda posters praised the development of the Soviet aviation industry as a major accomplishment of his first Five-Year plan. Subsequent posters were designed to build and maintain what he called "the enthusiasm essential to direct sacrifices of the masses into the proper organizational channel." [41]

---

[41] Soviet Aviation and Stalinism in the 1930's. See References.

Stalin promoted aviation as critical to industrial success

Stalin also realized he needed a ready supply of skilled pilots and support infrastructure. He promoted the concept of aero clubs, which historically had been the domain of wealthy enthusiasts. Stalin saw these clubs as flying schools where young pilots would train for entry into Red Army Air Force, as pilots, mechanics, technicians, glider pilots, and parachute jumpers. One such favored club, Aero Kalinin, located in Moscow, was popularized in the press as a place for male and female flyers to feed their enthusiasm.

Brothers from Ohio

Despite Stalin's desired version of history, one fact was irrefutable: two American brothers from the Midwest were the Fathers of Modern Aviation. They invented the machine that propelled man into the air, however briefly, for the first time.

A byproduct of that accomplishment was the publication of numerous biographies on the life and times of the two Midwest-born brothers.[42] One such biography was even translated into Russian and distributed in Soviet schools.

By the early 1940s every schoolchild in both America and Russia knew the names of the Wright Brothers. Newsreels and newspapers proudly talked of monuments erected in their name near the virtually unknown Kill Devils Hill on the Outer Banks of North Carolina, although few visited.

According to anecdotes of the time, a Russian language edition of the Wright Brothers' accomplishments inspired a Moscow teenager by the name of Lilia Litvyak to become the world's first female fighter pilot. During her short World War II career — she died 17 days before her 22nd birthday — she completed 268 missions, registered 15 solo kills, and assisted on 22 others. Those records still stand till this day.

---

[42] Wilbur was born in Midville, Indiana in 1867 and Orville in Dayton, Ohio in 1871.

The world's first female fighter-pilot, Lilia Litvyak (left),
plans a mission. Wright Brother's biography inset.

Why?

While the Wright Brothers themselves were well-known to the Soviets, little was known about how the Kitty Hawk site was selected. While in America, the Soviet Zebras were delighted to learn those details.

In 1900, a young mechanic named Wilber Wright, who had completed some research on Atlantic wind conditions, traveled by train from Ohio to Elizabeth City to observe the weather firsthand. He stayed at the old Arlington Hotel in downtown Elizabeth City for three days, waiting for a scheduled schooner ride to the Outer Banks. The 100-mile journey took three days because of inclement weather.

That would be the first of eight round-trips to Elizabeth City where the brothers purchased lumber, building materials, and other supplies to construct their airplane hangar and living quarters. [43]

---

[43] Legends of Elizabeth City. See References.

Circa 1900. Arlington Hotel, where the Wright Brothers slept.

First Requests

Given the Soviet fascination with flight, it was not surprising that every Soviet Zebra wanted to visit the Orville and Wilbur Monument located about 60 miles southwest of the Elizabeth City base. As Gagarin explained, "It wasn't a tourist trip; it was more of a religious pilgrimage to the Soviets."

Whenever there was "dull time" as the Soviets called it (no training, no planes, no weekends), Gagarin and Chernack would pile five or six of the Soviet officers into the Zebra station wagon and head down to the Outer Banks.

In those days, there were no tour buses, no souvenir stands, etc., just a long walk past a six-foot wide round dedication stone that ended at the top of one of the tallest sand dunes on the East Coast. On that spot stood a 60-foot pointed monument overlooking the Atlantic, which commemorated the exact spot where Orville and Wilbur's plane took off and landed for the first time.

Zebra officers at Wright Brothers monument on the hill

Cameras, Cameras

Before they left for the site, every Soviet Zebra made sure they had a camera and lots of film, purchased at The Apothecary on Main Street.

"To avoid tourists or questions, the men traveled mostly during the week," recalled Gagarin. "We only ran into a few locals once. They asked, 'Are those the Russian fellas we heard about?' I just nodded, and that was that."

After several trips, the orderly Zebras developed a process. After parking in the nearby sandy lot, the men would head directly to the monument and take tons of pictures. Then they'd light a cigarette, blow smoke puffs in the air, and breathe in the salty air. Nobody said much.

Smokes extinguished, they would rub the granite monument, then take a scoop of sand and throw it to the wind. "It was fascinating to see how important the place was to the men," said Gagarin. "Every so often, a Soviet official or translator from the Russian Embassy in Washington would join us. They rarely carried cameras but always found their way into the pictures, and asked their fellow countrymen to send copies to the Embassy."

Commander Chernack (lower left), Col. Chibisov (upper left),
and three senior Soviet officers

Once the Zebras had finished walking around the monument, they headed back to the dedication marker and took more pictures. On the way back to base, the car usually stopped at The Apothecary to drop off the film to be "rush" developed. Then they headed back to the Officer's Club for pre-dinner cocktails.

"Seventy-plus years later, whenever I look at the pictures," said Gagarin, " I recall those moments and the see the smiling faces of my Soviet friends. I can remember those hot and humid days when we were all thirsty; there wasn't a water fountain or a Coke machine to be found anywhere!"

(Today, the Kitty Hawk Museum Complex receives about 5 million visitors[44] a year, making it one of America's busiest tourist sites, with souvenir and Cokes for all).

---

[44] Dare County statistics. See References.

Chapter 23

Zebra Men's Club

American, Soviet, and RAF members of the Zebra Boys Club

As Project Zebra entered its second year, Chernack and Chibisov had gained a reputation for delivering expertly trained crews and well-maintained amphibious warplanes. The teams had developed mutual trust and professional respect that served them well during the inevitable downtimes.

Sometimes the Zebra teams had to await the arrival of new Soviet crews to train. Sometimes they had production lag times because the behemoth Nomads required large inventories of parts from third-party suppliers who were already working at full capacity. Initially, the Americans and Soviets passed the time separately. Eventually they came to enjoy doing things as a group, so the *Zebra Boys Club* was founded.

While the RAF was not officially part of the top-secret mission, Chernack and Chibisov agreed their contributions qualified them for "associate membership" in the club.

Horse Show

In the fall of 1944, Gagarin's father had called. He invited his son to judge a horse show at an elite girls' equestrian camp, Ecole Champlain in Vermont, where he had worked the past three summers.

Circa 1940s. Girls and instructors at Ecole Summer Camp

The young lieutenant quickly convinced Chernack to give him a weekend pass. Chernack asked, "And how do you plan to get there?"

Gagarin had his priorities. He wasn't going to fly anywhere without a qualified pilot. So he approached a highly skeptical Flickinger.

"How old are these girls?" asked Flickinger. "Is this another Grier?"

"This is a serious show," said Gagarin. "The riders are college freshman and sophomores, maybe older."

Flickinger decided to give his buddy one last chance. "Okay, I'll bite one more time, but..."

Gagarin now had a weekend pass and a pilot. All that was missing was a crew and a plane. Gagarin casually sat down next to Chibisov, who was having a cup of coffee at Zebra World Headquarters. "Good coffee, sir?"

"Better than Moscow," replied Chibisov who by now knew Gagarin was not much for small talk. "What do you want?"

Gagarin asked Chibisov if he could borrow one of *his* Nomads and invite some Soviets to crew the plane.

Chibisov smiled. "They are not *my* planes yet; I have not yet taken title. So, if you want my permission to fly *your* plane, I give it to you."

Chibisov agreed to let Gagarin ask his crews if anybody wanted to work the weekend — so long as they reported for duty at 1000 hours Monday morning, no excuses. Minutes after explaining the *Girls' Riding Show Mission*, Gagarin had a dozen volunteers.

Early Saturday morning, a giant Nomad with Red Stars and Russian characters flew up the Eastern seaboard, past Burlington, Vermont, and then made a wide turn toward the northern edge of Lake Champlain. A voice came over the radio from the nearby Montreal control tower. "Identify yourself. Markings unfamiliar."

Flickinger responded, "The markings are Russian, but we are…" The control tower shut down all two-way transmissions.

Soviet Nomad conspicuously sits on Lake Champlain, Vermont

As the Nomad descended, they noticed a bunch of pretty girls sunning themselves. Flickinger scanned the lineup. "We have arrived." He then gently flapped the wings as if to say hello. The girls looked up and waved.

One of the enlisted men threw a smoke bomb out of the plane. The sky filled with smoke. The girls giggled. The men knew it was going to be a fun-packed weekend.

Years later, Gagarin told his incredible Montreal-Lake Champlain story at a veterans' meeting. The obvious question arose: "How could you fly a giant plane with a Red Star up the coast and nobody challenged you?" Gagarin responded wryly, "In those days, people just never asked. I think I probably could have docked a German submarine in New York Harbor."

Sweet and Feisty

One of the girls on the beach that day was an attractive, well-bred lady named Ann. She had grown up around horses in Pennsylvania, so it was not surprising she attended Sweet Briar College for Girls, which excelled in both academics and equestrian programs.

She subsequently transferred and graduated from another elite school, Barnard College in New York City. She was working at Ecole for the summer because the senior Gagarin knew from experience that she was an outstanding equestrian who also spoke French fluently.

Shortly after Flickinger landed his plane on the Lake and ferried to shore, Gagarin and the crew were greeted by his father and three attractive camp counselors, one of which was Ann.

Getting to know you on Lake Champlain

At first, Ann said very little. She just looked at the tall officer as he made small talk with a few of the girls he had already dated. Years later, Ann recalled, "My first impression: he is handsome, but thinks he's God's gift to women."

As they sat and joked on the shores of Lake Champlain, Ann decided to bring the lieutenant down to earth — in a ladylike way. She said in French, "Hello, so pleased to meet you. Your Father often talks about you." The Lieutenant responded in kind. Ann was pleasantly surprised. "So, you speak some French?"

Gagarin smiled devilishly. "Well, let's just say I'm fluent in French, Russian, German, and English."

So much for Ann's plan! The couple spent the rest of the weekend getting to know each other in between judging sessions. The next evening, they attended a party at the school's cabin near the lake. "He held my hand so gently as we danced to my favorite song, 'I'll be Seeing You.'"

Later, Ann asked Greg if he would like to see her favorite place at Ecole: Eagles Rock. There, the couple watched the moonlight reflect off the lake for hours. In the blink of an eye, the weekend was over and the men flew back to Elizabeth, making a stop for "civilian" gas at the Burlington Airport so there would be no records in the log books.

Before Gagarin left, he asked Ann to marry him. She said, "I don't see why not."

Three dates and the deal was done

The couple corresponded in letters until the end of the war, when they eventually married.

Their wedding song? "I'll Be Seeing You."

The Blue Angel

Fall 1944. Gagarin's mom wanted to see her son, and Chernack and Flickinger wanted to see Manhattan. Gagarin's mother Elizabeth, a polished, internationally traveled person, worked at the Elizabeth Arden Salon on Fifth Avenue. She maintained a small apartment in Manhattan and lived at the family home in Long Island on weekends.

Flickinger insisted for *safety* purposes that they refuel at Consolidated Aircraft's facility in Queens, just miles from Manhattan. In Flickinger speak, *safety* meant he had Consolidated friends who would allow him to land and refuel without the need for messy logbook notations.

Chernack, Gagarin, and Gagarin's mother, Elizabeth,
at the Blue Angel Night Club in NYC

They met at one of Mom's favorite places, the Blue Angel Nightclub[45] on 55th Street off Third Avenue, which was also one of New York's most popular spots for drinks and jazz. By all accounts, the three had a great time, and Elizabeth shared some of the details of her son's youth — famous Russian heritage, born in Germany, raised in Paris, then to the states and MIT. It was the first time Chernack learned that Gagarin spoke fluent, Russian, French, German, and English.

Gagarin even shared a rare insight. "I remember when I was about eight years old in a French school, and the teacher asked me where I was from. I told him I wasn't sure. The fact was, I didn't even know my last name. I was just Grigori."

That evening, the Blue Angel had a new opening act: a young cabaret singer and pianist by the name of Bobbie Short. Gagarin's mom was taken by the way he placed sophisticated patter between songs. "She thought he had a chance to be a big nightclub star," said Gagarin.

---

[45] Chief of Naval Operations Chester Nimitz visited the club in 1946. He was so impressed he chose the name The Blue Angels for his world-famous acrobatic flying squadron.

Seeing a star before he was born

Years later, Short would become the most popular cabaret artist of the twentieth century. His home for over 30 years was the world-famous Carlyle Room on 76th Street and Madison Avenue, which was renamed Bobby Short Way in 2012, an honor usually reversed for royalty and world leaders.[46]

Water Street

As time went on, Chibisov came to realize that it might be difficult for future generations to believe the Project Zebra mission had really happened. "Given the strained relationships between our two countries," he wrote in his diary, "who would ever believe that the Americans trained our air force on American soil without asking for anything in return?" He urged his men to take pictures and to keep notes or diaries for family and loved ones since, as mentioned earlier, they were forbidden from sending detailed letters home.

While the American Zebras used their R&R to fly anywhere that sounded even remotely interesting, their Soviet counterparts felt more comfortable just spending their free time in Elizabeth City, unless accompanied by an English-speaking Zebra. The Soviet crews

---

[46] Bobby Short: Manhattan Icon. New York Times. See references.

especially liked the small restaurants and shops on Water Street, directly across from the harbor.

One day, Chibisov and Salnikov had taken themselves into town. To their amazement, a number of his well-groomed men in their dress blues were standing in front of a giant Nomad, in plain view. The enterprising crew had convinced two squads to drag the plane down the tarmac and into the river, then taxi to the park across from Water Street.

Russian pilots pose in the park near Water Street

Salnikov began to complain to Chibisov that the mission might be compromised, leading to "difficult personal consequences."[47] A smiling local photographer named Gordon Smith appeared with a camera. Somehow, the men had managed to hire him. As Smith lined the men up for a few test pictures, Chibisov walked across the street and began to admonish the men in Russian. Smith didn't understand a word, but the tone suggested that "the boss was mad as hell."

The men reminded Chibisov he had urged them "to make memories," and that the man had agreed to give them all the film after he took the pictures. Chibisov asked the photographer to stop.

---

[47] Diaries of Maxim Chibisov. See References.

Sometime later, Smith realized that in the confusion, nobody had asked for the film. He decided to see what he had, if anything. The above picture is the only known shot to have survived that photo session.

Virginia Dare

A town of 12,000 residents, Elizabeth City had only one building over three stories tall: the luxurious Virginia Dare Hotel,[48] named after the first child to be born in America of English parents, in 1587.

Virginia Dare lobby and bar: a Soviet Zebra weekend favorite

The Soviets didn't care about the hotel's history. They were more interested in the structure's two-story entrance and heated garage, with an interior filling station and a lubricating stand. They had never seen any such public hotel; it was a quintessential decadent capitalist structure the likes of which they had *heard* lined the streets of every American town and city.

They quickly learned about southern hospitality. The beautiful oak-paneled bar contained more types and brands of liquor than they had ever seen in one place. The bartender poured generous drinks,

[48] Coastal Carolina's tallest hotel. See References.

174

and the smiling patrons tried to make conversation with their Russian guests.

$2 Gamble

The two Soviet Captains asked the nightly price of a room. The bartender replied, "Two dollars per night." The captains decided to take a chance and stay overnight; the rest of the soldiers went back to the base.

When they went to their room, the captains were amazed to find two full-size beds with comfortable mattresses, attractive furnishings, and a private bath with both a shower and a soaking tub. "Better than home; maybe Comrade Stalin should see," said one.

Comfort and elegance at $2 per night

They went down for dinner. After struggling to order, they devoured juicy, well-aged ribeye steaks with all the fixings. When they asked for the bill, the waiter nodded but returned empty-handed. "Talked to the manager. He said tonight's on him."

The Soviets weren't quite sure what "on him" meant. Finally, the waiter became graphic. He took a dollar out of his pocket, ripped in half, stuffed it back in his pocket, and said, "Free, free."

The men smiled. "Da, da." They were pleased.

Then the manager approached the table. "Just our way of thanking you boys for coming such a long way. Don't know what the hell you guys are doing at the base; gotta be some top-secret deal. But you don't have to worry about this town; nobody will say anything to anybody." The men had no idea what the manager had said.

The dinner and drinks experience quickly spread around the base. Before long, the Virginia Dare became the Soviets' favorite weekend "field trip." The one free meal for two turned into hundreds of full-priced room nights over the next year or so.

Eastern Shore

As the Zebras trained over the Outer Banks and the Chesapeake Bay, they were amazed at the abundance of white sand beaches. They asked and received Chibisov and Chernack's blessings to explore the coastline by themselves. Looking at some maps, they traveled south past the Norfolk shipyards and turned around at the tip of the Chesapeake Bay.

Unknown to the Soviet crew, this caused quite a stir at the nearby Norfolk Naval base. Radar had identified a huge armed seaplane plane flying unannounced above the base. In seconds, gunsights were set on the target. The captain in charge asked for permission to fire if necessary. The commanding officer vaguely recalled a conversation with a Russian-American Naval officer assigned to Elizabeth City. He told everybody to hold tight while he called Chernack at Zebra World Headquarters.

"That's what I thought. No problem," said the commander. He then ordered his men to stand down. "It's just those Russian guys who are training in Elizabeth City." He laughed. "Imagine if those guys landed near the beach and had a picnic."

Soviet Zebras enjoy lunch near the sunny Chesapeake Bay

As the story goes, somewhere around the same time, the Soviet crew landed in the Bay and taxied to a quiet spot on the beach. There, they took a few pictures, had some sandwiches and beer, and enjoyed the afternoon sun.

When the Zebras returned, Chernack wanted to know more about the men's activities, in case he was asked to file a report. But none of the crew spoke English and Gagarin had gone to D.C. for the weekend.

Narragansett Island

Chernack was a master at motivating his men by modifying the rules to fit the behavior. Consequently, Gagarin was not surprised when Chernack asked him if he'd like to meet Edith and the kids on Narragansett Island. "You were nice enough to include me on Mom's trip in New York, so I thought I'd return the favor."

Next thing Gagarin knew, they were landing a four-seat, single-engine plane Chernack, which had been borrowed for the weekend from the Coast Guard base, on a small airstrip on Narragansett. Chernack described Narragansett as the perfect place to hide for a weekend.

As Gagarin recalled, they had a few cookouts — Chernack loved to barbecue — walked the beaches at sunset, and played a few board games with Chernack's kids in the evening. Gagarin also saw the unique bond between Chernack and his wife, Edith. "Don't know what I would ever do without her," Chernack said as he rocked in his chair on the porch.

Chernack and Gagarin relax at the commander's hideaway

As they flew back to base, Chernack winked. "Lieutenant, let's just keep this weekend between us. There are some things the boys don't need to know." Gagarin would keep Stanley's little secret for more than 70 years!

Chapter 24

Volleyball and V-E Day

The Zebra gymnasium was modest but functional. There were basketball courts at either end along with a volleyball court in the middle, which became the exercise of choice. Typically, the Americans batted the ball around on one side, the Soviets on the other.

Casual practice becomes a serious cultural challenge

One Saturday afternoon in early April, Chibisov suggested the two sides have a three-set match. At first, there was little interest. Finally, with some prodding, Gagarin was able to get commitments from five other officers to form a team. "We play tomorrow?" asked Chibisov.

"Da," replied Gagarin.

The Wager

Sunday came. Chibisov and his team arrived, dressed in form-fitting Soviet athletic shorts and shirts. "We are ready to play."

Flickinger whispered to Gagarin, "These guys look serious."

Chibisov said, "What we play for?"

"Sorry Colonel, we forgot about the game today. We don't have any rewards," smiled Gagarin, figuring that would end the challenge match before it began

Chibisov reached into his gym bag. "No problem. We bring rewards if you win." He took out a bouquet of red roses.

"We don't have a prize for your guys if we win," said Gagarin. "That's just not fair."

Chibisov paused and thought. "Have Plan B, as you Americans say." His proposal was both novel and culturally insightful. "If we win, you will buy vodka at the Club for a week. If we lose, we will carry the American flag in your independence celebration."

The Americans were reluctant. They had seen the Soviets drink; a week could get pricey. Gagarin saw it differently. There was no way a group of athletes like himself — he had captained the cross-country track team at MIT — could lose to the shorter, stockier Soviets. And he was intrigued by the potential reward. He had never seen a Soviet soldier carry an American flag anywhere, at any time.

Game time! Gagarin volunteered to play the setter position, while the rest of his mates argued about who should play outside and inside hitter, and middle and defensive specialist.

The Soviets formed a tight circle, did a series of high-fives, and then formed two lines. They executed a series of athletic stretches as the Americans watched and waited. Chibisov started moving players around. It quickly became apparent the moves had nothing to do with the game; he was organizing his men by some Soviet system of seniority and rank.

Big Trouble

It didn't take long for the Americans to realize they were in big trouble. A perfectly placed Soviet first serve whizzed by the outside hitter, untouched. Every ball the Americans managed to hit over the net was returned even faster. As Gagarin recalled, "It was like a bunch of high school kids playing a pro volleyball team."

The first set ended 21 to 10. The Americans were gassed, and they had no substitutes. Chibisov substituted fresh players in key positions. The second set was even worse: the Americans were forced to lunge at so many balls they could barely see through their sweat. The set final score was 21 to 8. The Americans looked at each and shook their heads in agreement. Gagarin approached Chibisov and said in Russian, "Okay, we give up. Let's shower and go to the club."

Vera Lynn entertains troops with WWII's favorite song

The Russians drank like fishes. It was now near closing time. Vera Lynn's "We'll Meet Again" began to play on the phonograph. The Americans and the Soviets started singing. When the song was over, Chibisov waved his men to the corner of the room. Everyone nodded. "It was like they took a vote," said Gagarin.

"I speak for the group," said the returning Chibisov. "When we end the war, we want to celebrate America on Victory Day. Something to tell our children."

Four weeks later, on May 8, 1945, Nazi Germany unconditionally surrendered to the Allied forces.

May 9, 1945

Elizabeth City was the perfect example of patriotic, small-town America. The Victory Day party in the center of downtown had candy, soda, smiles, kids, apple pie, and American flags. The high school band played the Star Spangled Banner. People put their hands on hearts and sang.

Mayor Jerome Flora made a few remarks about "the wonderful, blessed land that is America. A land worth fighting and dying for, so our freedoms can be passed on to future generations."

The mayor continued, "And I'd like to thank our Russian friends for their role in keeping the free, free." Flora paused, then surprised everyone — including Chibisov. "Colonel, would your men like to raise the flag in front of City Hall?" Chibisov was not quite sure what the mayor was asking. He turned to Gagarin, who translated.

Chibisov nodded and smiled. Soon, four Soviet officers in dress blues raised Old Glory in the air and posed for pictures in front of City Hall.

The photograph was published in the Elizabeth City Daily Advance the next day. To the best of this author's knowledge, this photograph is the only time in history that Russian soldiers hoisted the American flag on American shores. It is not known if anyone in the USSR or Russia has ever seen this historic picture.

VOLUME XXXV—NO. 112.   FINAL EDITION

Russian Allies Raise Flag in Elizabeth City

*Circa 1944. The only time in history that Russian soldiers hoisted the
American flag on American shores.*

Chapter 25

Hobo News

Fire and Brimstone Conservative vs Populist Social Champion

Much of Project Zebra took place during the heat of the 1944 presidential election between polished, three-term Democrat incumbent Franklin Roosevelt, and the intense and the at times incendiary Republican nominee, Thomas Dewey, a former New York district attorney.

Since Dewey was a long shot, his strategy was to support themes he thought would disturb the populist status quo. His platform promised to strip away the inefficiency and corruption in Roosevelt's New Deal programs and eliminate the menace of communism he saw as attempting to seize control of the federal government under Roosevelt's rule. Neither platform held much traction, as Dewey gathered only 45% of the popular vote and lost the electoral college by the astounding margin of 432-99.

The anti-communist vitriol disturbed Chibisov, who was proud to lead the Soviet side of Project Zebra. As a person who knew only the communist way, he was stunned at the public skewering of a political leader.

Private Talks

An avid reader and internationalist, Chibisov read the popular daily Russian language newspaper *Novoye Slovo* (New Day) and listened intently to Russian radio that was broadcast from New York.

Because the name of the paper in Cyrillic looked much like the American letters H-O-B-E, the Americans decided to call the paper the *Hobo News*. The Russians never understood why the name seemed so funny.

Hobo News. Published in America. By Russians.

One day in early October, Chibisov summoned his friend Gagarin for a "private talk." Gagarin had learned by now that Chibisov never discussed his feelings during training sessions or over drinks at the officers' club. When Chibisov had a cultural question, he would ask Gagarin — because of both his fluency and men's growing friendship — to take a walk aside the runway. While the runway was in public view, Chibisov was confident there were no secret recording devices present. Both men knew that in Stalin's Russia, you could never be sure of whom you could trust; stories of friends ratting on friends were not uncommon.

This day, Chibisov wanted to talk about the report of a rousing rally in Boston where Dewey labeled communism as "a pagan philosophy supported by Roosevelt, designed to eliminate freedom of religion, abolish civil rights, [and] eliminate personal savings and property ownership."

Gagarin assumed Chibisov was offended by the rhetoric about his homeland. Chibisov explained he was not talking about communism; he was talking about Roosevelt, the American president who had helped his country.

"Do all Americans believe what Dewey says?"

"I can't speak for everybody, but Americans are free to say what they think."

"Should Dewey win, could Zebra be canceled?"

"I really don't think Dewey has much of a chance," said Gagarin.

"So why does Roosevelt say such things about him? Why do they let Dewey say such things? You know in Russia, Dewey could not say such things about Comrade Stalin," said Chibisov. "He would be arrested and sent to a labor camp. What happens is this man Dewey loses the election?"

"I guess he'll probably go and find another job," replied Gagarin.

Chibisov stared blankly.

Always Share

On another occasion, the two men discussed political systems.

"How do you explain the American system?" asked Chibisov.

"In our society, people believe they work to enjoy life. Everyone has an equal opportunity to fulfill their dreams though their own efforts." explained Gagarin.

Chibisov replied, "I have been taught differently. One works for the benefit of all. And all have the same."

"Does your system work?" asked Gagarin.

"For the most part," said Chibisov. "Sharing is the Russian way of life."

Six Moscow families shared one kitchen in Stalin's world

As the months passed, Chibisov came to see the benefits of the American system firsthand: the endless variety of goods in the stores, even during wartime; the happy faces of small town America; and the willingness of everybody to accept him and his countrymen as friends who should be treated with respected. Capitalism was not a monster to be avoided at all costs.

Occasionally, after some of their walks, Chibisov would retire to his room and make notations in his diary. Only once did Gagarin ask what he wrote about in his book. Chibisov responded in imperfect English, "I write to remember these times when I return home and the years pass and my memory fades."

Chapter 26

French Perfume

Soviets' favorite store for shaving equipment and sundries

In 1925, childhood friends John Stevenson and Harold Overman decided their hometown needed a local pharmacy. They opened the doors to Overman & Stevenson Druggists on Main Street in the center of town, where it has continued to thrive for more 90 years.

When the Navy expanded its Elizabeth City base during World War II, the store became the soldier's choice for day-to-day sundries like shaving equipment.

John's son Paul, today's current owner, was about 11-years-old when the Japanese attacked Pearl Harbor. Too young to enlist, he worked part time after school at the pharmacy because every able-bodied young man was off fighting in the war.

At first, he just moved inventory from the delivery trucks to the stock room and cleaned the place up after closing. Within two years, he was filling display cases and waiting on customers. "Dad said I had 'the gift of gab.' But I just liked people."

One day in early 1944, Paul saw a group of six to eight soldiers in unfamiliar dark blue uniforms walking up Main Street, laughing and playfully pushing and shoving each other. "People just stopped in their tracks. Elizabeth City has always been a quiet, conservative little town, so the boys really stood out," smiled Paul.

Next thing Paul knew, the men pointed to the pharmacy sign and entered. Paul's dad Nick walked up to them. At first, neither party could bridge the language gap.

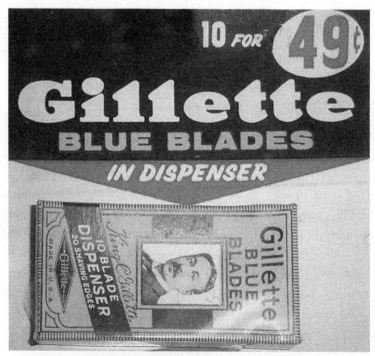

Soviets knew certain American brands

One of the soldiers walked to the counter and started rubbing his hand on his face. Nick stared. The man pointed to a shelf: "Gillette, Gillette."

Nick placed a package of blue Gillette razor blades on the counter. Two more soldiers rubbed their faces. Two more packages. Another cupped his hand, then rubbed the other in it. Nick was stumped. "Dad," said Paul, "why not put an assortment of shaving supplies on the counter and let them choose?" Nick smiled at his son's ingenuity. Each soldier then selected what they wanted by holding up a product and signaling with their fingers.

Paul recalls that first meeting with the Soviets

When the process was complete, there were seven piles of shaving supplies on the counter — one for each soldier. Nick scribbled the costs on a pad for each soldier. The process was time-consuming and noisy. By the time the soldiers finished, every customer and employee was watching the show.

"The soldiers handed my father some American dollars. They gave him too much, so he tried to explain and give them change.

They didn't understand. They thought he was rejecting the currency. All they could say was 'Americanish. Good.' Even I had to laugh. Somehow, the purchases were completed and they began to leave. The last one saw our perfume counter not far from the front door. He pointed, 'French?' My father nodded. The soldier shouted to his friends. They all returned.

"He began to point at the French brands. Dad asked if anyone wanted a test spray. They had no idea what he was talking about. One of the clerks, an attractive young lady by the name of Pearl, took a tester bottle of Jean Naté and sprayed it on her wrist. Then she held it close to one of the soldiers and said, 'Ooh la la.'"

Brands of choice: Au du Temps, Maguey, Jean Naté

Soon Pearl was surrounded by the six men. Each wanted to try a fragrance. She was patient and friendly as each one held a different shaped bottle and sprayed their wrists. When everybody had tested each brand, the men huddled and began to talk loudly in Cyrillic. Everybody gave their money to one soldier, who stepped forward. Pearl figured he had been nominated to order for the group. He pointed to the row of Jean Naté boxes. Pearl placed a box on the counter. The man shook his head, made a big circle with his arms, and then closed them.

Pearl nodded. She put every bottle of Jean Naté in stock on the counter. The soldier smiled and then pointed to the row of Au Du Temps perfume. "French?" Pearl nodded. Again, she stacked every box on the counter.

"Daddy and I were amazed. Pearl somehow figured out they wanted every bottle of French perfume we had in stock. After the money changed hands, they loaded everything into this blue bus with a Navy seal. The driver, an American officer with a foreign accent [probably Chief Ski], smiled. 'We just finished *training* these men at the base. They probably just wanted a few souvenirs for their wives and girlfriends before they go fight the Nazis.'"

Nick Stevenson was curious. He now knew there were Russians in Elizabeth City, but he had no idea what 'training' meant. He also knew the soldiers purchased a lot of perfume... for wives and girlfriends. He told the French perfume story to a few of his merchant friends at Comstock's Confectionery over an ice-cream cone. Nobody had any idea what the Russians did at the base. "Dad told me the whole thing seemed mysterious. But it was wartime and better to not ask too many questions."

In time, Elizabeth City retailers realized that when 'one of those' Russian crews was about to return to the Soviet Union, they came to town and stocked up on branded goods. The rumor was the soldiers packed all the stuff on planes and resold it in Moscow and Leningrad at a hefty profit.

After the 'Gillette' incident, Nick Stevenson made sure his pharmacy was stocked with lots of French perfume whenever he heard the Russians were about to leave. "He even asked our wholesaler if he carried any more French brands. Before long, I was adding Channel, Jontue, Shalimar, and Tabu to our shelves.

"Our regular customers couldn't help but notice the increased variety. As one put it, 'shopping at Stevenson's these days is like Christmas come early.'"

Chapter 27

Human Error

Circa 1944. Consumer store shelves stocked to the brim.

Whenever a new group of Soviet Zebras came to Elizabeth City, they wanted to visit the food stores they had heard so much about from the others. They couldn't believe one store could carry five cereal brands, as well as multiple flavors and types of jelly, jam, and preserves.

When the Nazis invaded Russia, Stalin had implemented strict rationing of virtually all consumer items. Nevertheless, most Soviet citizens handled these challenges with stoic determination, personal workarounds, and a uniquely Russian sense of humor.

Mom's Funeral

A familiar Soviet World War II story spoke to these emotions.

"My 84-year old mother died," said Irina. (Under Soviet law, the deceased and their family were guaranteed a free funeral and burial.)

"First stop was the morgue, where I was told that the burial spaces were filled. When I paid 100 rubles to the attendants, they found a space. Of course, there was an extra 25 rubles for mother's shroud.

"The funeral agent told me there were no coffins for a five-foot woman, only eight-feet long coffins. For 40 rubles, the agent found the right size.

"The gravediggers then told me they could not dig the grave until 2:00 P.M., even though mother's funeral was at 10:00 A.M. I again found a solution to the problem: two bottles of vodka plus 15 rubles for each gravedigger."

"Even transportation posed problems. "The driver of the funeral bus told me he had another funeral that day, so he couldn't take care of us. For 15 rubles and another bottle of vodka, I solved that problem. And so on with the flowers and all the rest.

"In the end, it cost 800 rubles to bury my mother — about three months' income for our entire family."[49]

Radio Discovery

January 10, 1945. The delivery of the next 100 planes through the Southern Route (see Chapter 11) had gone smoothly. The final squadron was scheduled to leave the following evening. As usual, the intermediate legs would be flown by RAF pilots, and land at South American and African RAF bases. There, they would be turned over to all-Soviet crews as they traveled the last leg into Soviet airspace.

Hours before they left, the Russian pilot, co-pilot, and navigator tested all the specialized electronics, because they knew Gagarin would not be coming along to advise or guide them. They quickly realized the radio system wasn't working and asked Gagarin to help. When he arrived, Gagarin asked the exact nature of the problem. The Soviets responded animatedly in Russian. Gagarin nodded calmly

---

[49] Russian Shadow Economy. See References.

and entered the plane. By now, there were a dozen concerned crew members and trainers surrounding the plane.

Gagarin asked the pilot in front to say something to the navigator in the rear of the plane. The pilot pressed the call button on the back of the seat. Silence. Gagarin went to the navigator in the rear. And asked him to do the same thing, to call the pilot. The navigator pressed his call button. Again, silence.

Gagarin returned to the front. The button behind the seat was in the off position. He told the pilot to turn it on and leave it on. Gagarin returned to the rear and noticed the navigator button was also off. He told him to "leave it on." He returned to the front and told the pilot to call the navigator. Problem solved. Gagarin explained precisely how the Nomad's two-way communication worked then issued simple instructions: "On takeoff, turn the radio on. When you land, turn the radio off."

As Gagarin got off the plane, everybody applauded. He walked over to Chibisov and Chernack. "Gentlemen, I think we have a bigger problem."

The Commanders stared blankly. Gagarin continued, "As I fixed the nonproblem, I almost broke my neck climbing over cases of cigarettes, coffee, and booze, and bolts of fabric. It's like a PX in there. I could be wrong, but the plane may be too heavy to climb properly."

Chibisov wouldn't accept Gagarin's conclusion. He explained that the men had been away from their family for months, had worked hard in an unfamiliar land, and were about to go into battle against the vicious Germans. It was only fair that they bring home goods that they and their families could enjoy, sell, and barter with on the secondary market. He paused. "I know both of you have Russian blood, but you don't know Russian life. You cannot imagine the difficulties. These goods will let many Russian people enjoy what you Americans take for granted."

Gagarin looked at the weather forecast: crystal clear skies and still air. What could he say? The crews had navigated their route many times during training exercises and would be captained by an

English-speaking pilot for thousands of miles. Gagarin left for the weekend to visit friends in the Washington, D.C., area.

Tragic Flight

At 8:00 P.M. (2000 hours) the following day, the huge plane, its enormous cargo, and a crew of nine — one Brit, a Canadian, and seven Russians — lifted itself off the water and followed the light created by the kerosene-light buoys. As the pilot passed the last flare, he attempted to increase his speed and altitude. Suddenly, the plane began to shudder. The pilot looked at his altimeter and then radioed, "Unable to rise. Unable to rise!" He was advised to return to base. That was the last transmission before the plane crashed and disappeared.

According to the RAF pilot's statement later, he lost sight of the horizon and misjudged the radius needed to turn the plane around. When he realized the mistake, the RAF pilot explained he tried to raise the nose of the plane, but the engine failed.

Officially, the cause of the crash was listed as human error. However, given Gagarin's clear recollection that the plane was significantly overweight due to additional cargo, no one will ever know for sure exactly which type of human error was involved.

Official Reports

During the ensuing search mission in the dark, choppy waters, the British pilot and three Russian crew members were rescued. One day later, on January 12, the government issued a confidential report (below) regarding the crash. It listed four survivors and six missing in action. The report also stated, "further details to follow."

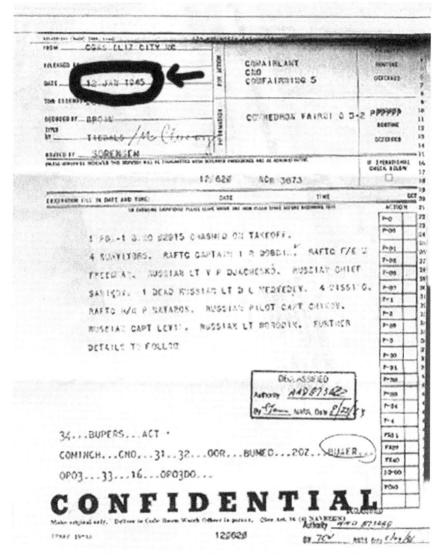

Confidential US memo documents the tragic incident

Since the mission remained top secret, there were no subsequent press stories, no further discussion at the base, and no additional government details.

The bodies of the other five crew members — Captain Vladimir M. Levin; Russian aviators Afanasie Borodin Sr., D.M. Medvedev, and H.N. Chisov; and a Canadian radio operator, Peter Nataros, were never found and presumed dead. According to the five death certificates certified by Dr. Grover Moore of the U.S.N and issued at the Pasquotank County Courthouse, the men died at approximately 8:05 P.M. (2005 hours) approximately five minutes after takeoff.

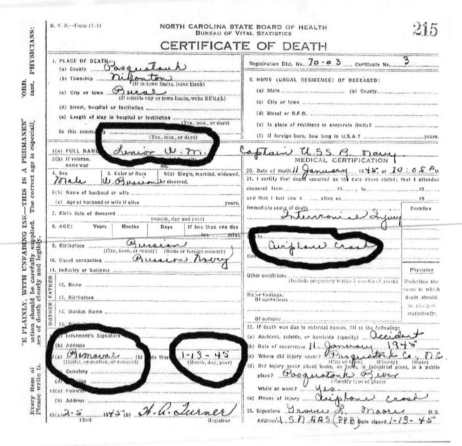

Death certificate states the deceased were victims of a plane crash

On October 8, 1945, almost seven months after the crash, the family of one of the men killed in the crash, Captain Vladimir Levin from Odessa, Ukraine, received an official government notice that their son had died trying to save an American officer during an undisclosed military maneuver.

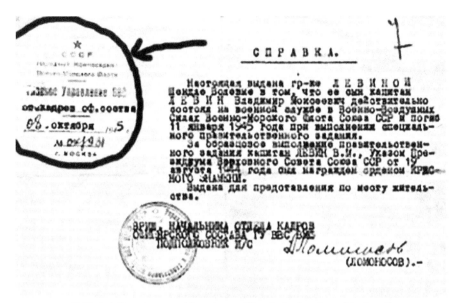

Official Russian notification of Levin's death to his family

Seeking Closure

At the site of the crash, the water was about 20 feet deep. Yet despite numerous rescue operations, traces of the actual plane have never been found. According to Elizabeth City Mayor Joe Peel, "The shore line has eroded some sixty feet since those days, so it's a pretty safe assumption that plane is buried under hundreds of tons of silt and sand."

Another issue is the deposition of the bodies. According to the Certificates of Death, the body of each soldier was "removed." But to this day, there is not one clue about where or how.

The most solemn public holiday in Russia is known to simply as May Day: the end World War II. The USSR lost an estimated 40 million people during the war.[50] That number is greater than all the lives lost by all the other allies combined, including Holocaust victims. On May 9, 2015, Russia celebrated the 70th anniversary of May Day.

---

[50] Soviet Casualties of War. See Reference.

In the spirit of final closure, the World-Wide Club of Odessites based in Odessa, Ukraine, sent a letter to the mayor of Elizabeth City, the Honorable Joseph Peel, on June 14, 2014, hoping someone could shed some light on what happened to Captain Levin. The club hoped to gain closure for the family in time for the 70th anniversary commemoration. Unfortunately, for whatever reason, the letter never reached his desk.

Capt. Vladimir Levin, 23, the handsome Odessa crew member

Всемирный клуб одесситов
ул. Маразлиевская, 7 Одесса 65014
Украина
Тел/Факс +38(048)725-53-68, 725-45-67.
E-mail: vko@list.ru
www.odessitclub.org

World-Wide Club of Odessites
7, Marazlievskaya st., Odessa 65014
Ukraine
Tel/Fax +38(048)725-5368, 725-4567
E-mail: vko@list.ru
www.odessitclub.org

Mr. Joseph W. Peel
Mayor
P.O. Box 347
Elizabeth City, NC
27907-0347
USA

Re: WWII lend-lease aircraft crash

June 19, 2014

Dear Mr. Peel,

My addressing you stems from the fact that two our cities appeared related through a WWII accident.

11 January 1945 *Catalina* PBN-1 02915 aircraft crashed on take off from the Elizabeth City, NC (and sank in Pasquotank River) on its route to Habbaniah, Iraq (the first leg of the lend-lease ferry route). Five deaths were registered at Nixonton, Pasquotank County.

Among those above was a Russian pilot, **Odessa citizen** Captain Vladimir (Valentin) M. Levin.

Letter of request from Ukraine to the Mayor of Elizabeth City.

Chapter 28

Nomads at Work

Circa 1945. Soviet rendering: Nomad destroys German U-boat

Long before Pearl Harbor, the Soviets astutely recognized their navy needed a long range, battle-capable seaplane. So in 1938, the Soviets contracted with the Consolidated Aircraft Company to produce a modified version of its popular Catalina "Flying Boat" seaplane in a factory in Taganrog, Russia, a seaport city about ten miles from the border of Southern Ukraine. During Operation Barbarossa, the German military overtook the city and the aircraft factory, effectively eliminating seaplanes from the Soviet Naval fleet. By late 1942, only five Soviet flying boats were marginally functional. Fortunately, or unfortunately, during this period, seaplanes played a negligible role in the war because the decisive Nazi-Soviet battles in 1942 and 1943 were all land-based.

Catalina on Steroids

This land focus gave America the time needed to modify, produce, and deliver a Nomad flying boat. It had an enlarged fuel tank that increased the original Catalina range by 50 percent; increased ordnance payloads; upgraded machine gun turrets with reliable, continuous-feed mechanisms; and a next-generation radar system that identified underwater activity at greater distances.

As the Allies took to the offensive in early 1944, the Soviet Nomads served three initial functions: first, to escort sea convoys to protect weapon shipments and other needed supplies; second, to lead seek-and-destroy missions in the rough North Atlantic seas, to improve kill-ratios of German subs and U-Boats; and finally, to identify enemy watercraft, to improve the accuracy of strategic bombing raids.

By February 1945, more than 125 Nomads had seen military action. Because Project Zebra was top-secret, Chibisov never received any formal written reports about battlefield performance. However, the word-of-mouth feedback from those pilots who had delivered the planes and trained others to fly them was overwhelmingly positive.

Soviet crews were enthusiastic about the Nomad's ability to complete multiple maritime patrol missions without refueling. As the distinguished Nomad pilot Nikolay Zaytsev[51] recalled years later, "What can I say about our Allied machine? It seemed the plane that could stay in the air forever without refueling. Nobody had anything like it."

Zaytsev also appreciated the flying boats' advanced radar. "We found it could identify enemy ship locations at distances of 120 miles. This was a distinct advantage during our many night missions. Our magnificent radar system remained on duty twenty-four hours a day. We were fortunate to be one of the seventy-five." [52]

---

[51] Winner of the Hero of Soviet Union award.

[52] Due to parts shortages, it is estimated about half of the Nomads had the advanced radar systems.

Norden Bombsight

The United States equipped 125 of the Nomads that traveled the South American and Alaskan routes with a top-secret, deadly accurate bombsight called Norden, previously only used by American B-17 bombers.

The sight contained two principal parts: an extremely accurate sight head and a heavy-duty stabilizer. Once the target was identified, autopilot took the plane to the precise location where the bombs were to be released. The sight head, and its accompanying assembly, increased the accuracy of dropped bombs by an estimated 100 percent. To maintain peak performance, the sights were stored in air-conditioned, dust-proof vaults until installed on the planes.

The Norden was considered so top-secret that USAAF bombardiers had to swear a solemn oath to guard the weapon with their lives. There was significant concern among the military command about giving this technology to an unpredictable ally like the USSR. In the end, it was decided that eliminating Hitler now was more important than what *might* happen at some point in the future.[53]

Soviet Zebra train on state-of-the-art Norden bombsights

Since this bombsight was completely unknown to the Soviets, there were intensive classroom and simulator sessions moderated by

---

[53] The top-secret Norden bombsight. See References.

a Zebra ordnance specialist who also spoke Russian. Class sessions were followed by simulated bombing exercises. Hypothetical enemy locations were identified in Albemarle Sound, where dummy bombs were dropped day and night.

When the military exercises concluded, the sights were stored in a secret location only known by a small team of American Zebras. No mention was ever made to departing Zebras about solemn oaths.

Payload Advantages

Other positive feedback recounted the amount and types of ordnance on board the Nomads.

Nomad pilot Sergey Pasechnik recalled that his crew was often tasked with escorting ships of the Soviet Black Sea Fleet. "During convoy escort, we had to carry 16 depth charges on each Nomad," Pasechnik stated, "but we never had a chance to use them — the German submarines were afraid of us."

On another occasion, Zebra Captain S.M. Rubana and his crew were on a reconnaissance mission, traveling without depth charges. Suddenly he crossed paths with a German submarine, which began firing furiously. To the submarine's surprise, Rubana's Nomad returned the fire using all eight of his Browning .50 caliber machine guns. The sub began to descend. By this time, two more Nomads, each armed with depth charges, arrived and proceeded to drop their ordnance. The crews of all three Nomads saw a stream of oil rising to the surface, making it the first successful Soviet Nomad attack against a German submarine. The incident convinced German submarines that the heavily-armed Soviet flying boats posed a threat significant enough to warrant submerging when Nomads were in the area.

During the Zebra training in North Carolina, it was impossible to fire rounds from the machine gun turrets. So when Chibisov received word of their battlefield performance, he was pleased. Gunner Sergei Lyubov even made a few notations in his wartime notes: "They were wonderful machine guns that never jammed in all my service. It was a reliable and effective weapon. Enjoy doing again sometime soon."[54]

Soviet Reports[55]

According to additional Russian documents, the first Nomad combat mission was on June 18, 1944, when it traveled through enemy airspace to rescue the crew of a Soviet ground attack aircraft IL-2, which had been forced to hand in in Norway.

Other report highlights include:

The initial squadron of Nomads was used in the North Atlantic to detect enemy submarines and floating mines along convoy routes in the Barents Sea, the White Sea straits, and parts of the Kara Sea.

Nomads were used to rescue entire crews of sunken Soviet surface ships in the Atlantic and Pacific Theaters, and even sank an enemy training battleship docked in Poland during a night raid.

Spetsnaz

In time, the Red Navy found an additional, less-conventional role for these flying boats: transporting special commando forces, called Spetsnaz, to strategic sites on the Danube that were unreachable by other aircraft.[56] There, these specially trained operatives would complete stealth disruptive nighttime raids against Axis encampments. In most cases, the heavily-armed Nomads carrying squads of Spetsnaz operatives would land, complete their sabotage mission, and then disappear in the dark skies before the enemy had a chance to regroup and retaliate.

---

[54] Blood on the Shores. See References.

[55] Reports of Rear Admiral Boris G. Novyy, Retired Federation Navy. See references.

[56] Spetsnaz was an early Soviet version of U.S. Navy Seals

Soviet commando, Viktor Leonov, lionized in war poster

Viktor Leonov,[57] the Soviet's most legendary commando operative, recalled the Nomads' role in restoring the Bulgarian Government. "Approximately August 29 to September 8, 1944, our Nomads landed commando units near Varna — the strategically important Bulgarian port on the Black Sea." After continued raids, the frustrated Nazis retreated and a Communist government was reinstalled. A similar Spetsnaz operations took place in Denmark in 1945. It appears that about 15 Nomads took part in these secret operations during 1944-45. According to Leonov, "Spetsnaz never lost a commando or a single Nomad."[58]

---

[57] Named Hero of Soviet Union twice, an award like the American Purple Heart.

[58] Blood on the Shores. See References.

Nomads in the Pacific

Before and during WWII, the Japanese owned and occupied the Kuril Islands chain, which began less than ten miles off the coast of Russia on the innermost island of Sakhalin.

An avowed enemy ten miles from The Homeland.

Consequently, deliveries of Lend-Lease equipment did not stop with the capitulation of Germany in May 1945. Western Allies knew the Red Army still had to protect the Homeland against a Pearl-Harbor-style Japanese invasion. Under the terms of Lend-Lease, America produced hundreds more P-63 King Cobra fighter planes and 50 more Nomads for the Pacific Theater. By August 9, when the Soviet Union formally entered the war against Japan, the Soviet Pacific Fleet had 71 Nomads.

These last Nomads saw extensive military action during this last phase of the War — performing anti-submarine missions; search-and-rescue operations; and troop transportation, most notably airborne troops during the South Sakhalin and the Kuril Landing Operation in August and September. As part of the subsequent terms of surrender, Sakhalin became part of the Soviet Union. (Today it is connected by rail to the mainland.) Ironically, in modern times, the Japanese and Russians have been discussing the construction of a 27-mile Sakhalin–Hokkaido Bridge Tunnel.[59]

One PBN disappeared during the Far East Campaign, accounting for the Soviet Union's only lost flying boat during the Soviet-Japanese War of 1945.[60]

Unexpected Complement
As Project Zebra ended, the Soviet officer in charge of Nomad production, Colonel Tiertsiev, decided to write Commander C.E. Szekely, the Naval Aircraft Factory's Production Superintendent. The letter reinforced anecdotal plane performance and demonstrated that the dry, witty Soviet sense of humor remained alive and well. Tiertsiev wrote the letter in English and Russian, presumably to provide a copy to his commanding officer in the Homeland. Key passages read:

The PBN's [sic] have been received in Russia with keen enthusiasm, where no time is lost getting them into combat...

Our pilots are pleased with their performance, stamina and sturdiness. Although they have occasionally been shot-up a little, they have always retuned...

We know your untiring efforts have allowed us to receive double and triple the original order. Although we don't pretend to know how this great feat was accomplished, we are deeply grateful for it...

---

[59] World's longest train tunnel: Gottard, Switzerland, 67 miles. See References.

[60] Soviet Catalina's of WW II. See references.

Commander O. E. Szekely,
Production Superintendent,
Naval Aircraft Factory,
Philadelphia Navy Yard,
Philadelphia, Pennsylvania.

Dear Commander Szekely:

As the PBN draws to a close, I would like to express our deep appreciation of your part in this....

The PBN's have been received in Russia with keen enthusiasm where no time is lost in getting them into combat service. In one instance, a PBN was sent into combat just four hours after arrival. Our pilots are pleased with their performance, stamina and sturdiness in combat. Although they have occasionally been shot-up a little, they have always returned. We know that these good qualities of sturdiness and performance are in large measure the result of your careful supervision of their production.

On this side, we know that it is through your untiring efforts that the production schedule for PBN's has been not merely maintained but doubled and almost tripled. Although we don't pretend to know how this great feat was accomplished, we are greatly impressed by it and deeply grateful for it.

On behalf of myself my predecessors in command here at Elizabeth City, and our pilots and crews, I wish to thank you from the bottom of my heart for the wonderful work you have done in producing such fine aircraft and in getting the job done so quickly.

Respectfully yours,

Lt. Col. V. A. TERTSEV
Commander, Elizabeth City Detachment,
U.S.S.R. Naval Air Forces

Luxury Flight

The ability of Catalina amphibious crafts to remain aloft for extraordinary lengths of time did not go unnoticed by the commercial airline industry. Qantas Imperial Airways[61] purchased three luxury passenger-friendly Catalinas from the Consolidated plant in San Diego, California, during the war. From June 1943 to June 1945, Qantas scheduled non-stop flights between Perth, Australia, and

---

[61] Today Qantas Imperial Airlines is known simply as Qantas Airways.

Colombo, Ceylon, [62] traversing the Indian Ocean. But ultimately, operating costs outstripped demand and the route was abandoned.

Luxury flying: 38 passengers, crew of 12.

The pitch for those who could afford the premium price was "Speed with Spacious Comfort: Sleeping Areas. Smoking Room, Promenade Deck." At the time, they were the longest flights in the history of commercial aviation. The Qantas flying boat traveled 3,592 miles nonstop, which took 28 to 32 hours.

---

[62] Now Sri Lanka.

Chapter 29

Goodbye America

Soviet Zebras receive details of their return home

Late summer, 1945. Everyone knew Project Zebra was coming to a close. Some of the Soviets were understandably homesick, some were not, and some wished they could make a few more shipments of black market goods.

For Gagarin and Chibisov, the emotions were a bit different. Gagarin had been a bit of a celebrity among the Soviets because of his well-known family name and his social position as a prince. He was going to miss the familiar Russian request of "Prince, please help me."

Chibisov rarely spoke about his personal feelings in public, but it was clear to Gagarin and the others that Chibisov liked America; it was much different from what he had been led to believe, in so many ways. "Everything in America is just easier to do," was a familiar refrain.

Privately, Chibisov recognized America would be a wonderful place to raise a family and live in peace and prosperity after the war.

"He only said it one time," recalled Gagarin. "'Could live here. America very good, but I am Russian. My family is Russian. My roots are Russian.'" Gagarin always wondered, but never asked, why Chibisov never called himself Soviet.

Smiling Economy

For most of the Soviet Zebras — including counterintelligence agent Major Salnikov — one of their most vivid postwar memories would be the robust American economic machine.

When they first arrived in America, they knew only what they had been taught: American capitalism was decadent; only a state-dominated, globally-isolated, centrally-planned economy could improve their quality of life and keep the State strong and vital.

But decadent capitalism was not the reality they had experienced during the last 18 months. Despite the fact that there was a major war underway, the store shelves were full, and even though Americans shared through a system of rationing, there were no long lines outside the shops.

"The thing that simply amazed the Soviets," recalled Gagarin, "was the openness of the people and creativity of our capitalist economy despite the tumultuous times."

One evening, not long before the mission's end, the perpetually dour Salnikov and Tiertsiev, made several toasts at the Officer's Club to southern hospitality and the American way. But they were careful never to declare such sentiments in writing. They knew reporting such an observation could lead to re-education in a Soviet labor camp.

The following morning, those Zebras who had been ordered to return home first stood on the shore with their rifles and duffel bags draped over their shoulders. They waited for the boat to ferry them to the belly of a Nomad, where they would become passengers on a flight that would make stops in Newfoundland and Iceland, before finally landing in northern Russia.

"Little was said. I could see my men were both happy to be going home to loved ones and sad to leave so many good friends. At that moment, I wondered what the future might hold for our two countries and our different ways of life. I could only hope that history might one day show our children and our grandchildren there was a moment in time that should be repeated."[63]

Tiffany's

Chernack told Gagarin he had been thinking about getting Chibisov a going away present, something to help him remember his experience in America. Noting that Chibisov was a heavy smoker, he suggested an engraved sterling silver cigarette case. Gagarin was surprised at such a grand gesture. "Not going to find one of those at the PX in Norfolk."

Chernack explained he was thinking of one of the high-end jewelry stores in New York. "Ask your mother," he told Gagarin. He remembered Gagarin's mother was "quite the lady about Manhattan."

Chernack shops for a going away present

Elizabeth Gagarin didn't hesitate, "Tiffany's on Fifth, and they engrave for free." Gagarin passed the information along. He never asked Chernack when he planned to go shopping or how he was going

---

[63] Diaries of Maxim Chibisov. See References.

to pay for the case. Gagarin was confident that Chernack — like Chief Ski — was quite resourceful!

The following week, Chernack took Gagarin aside and took a blue Tiffany felt bag out of his pocket. He showed Gagarin the handsome sterling silver cigarette case with the initials "M.C." engraved on the front. "So, what do you think?"

Gagarin nodded his approval. "Good," said Chernack, "glad you like it. Now it's your job to get the signatures of all our officers on the card that will accompany the case."

Farewell Bash

The next weekend, the Soviets were to depart by Navy DC-4s to Anchorage, Alaska, where they would take title to the last delivery of Nomads from the Americans. Chernack suggested they have a little going away bash.

After dinner at the officer's club, the festivities began. Chernack rose from his seat first. He made the obligatory comments about teamwork and allies working together for the common good. Then he asked Chibisov to step forward, and Chernack presented him with the cigarette case. Chibisov was clearly moved when he opened the case and saw all the signatures.

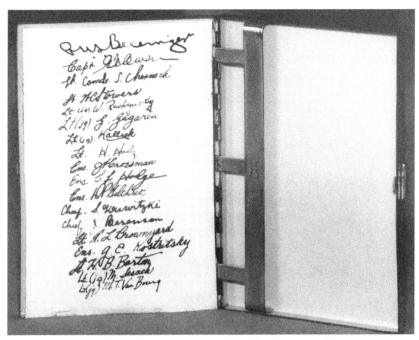

The sterling silver case signed by the American Zebras

"We also wanted to make sure you don't run out of smokes back in ration-land," teased Chernack as he pulled a case of Camel cigarettes from under the table.

Then it was Chibisov's turn. He said in his best English, "You know Russians are poor; we don't have capitalist gifts. But we understand kindness. You have all you done much for our country, so we have some Soviet gifts."

Chibisov paused and looked at Gagarin. "For my good friend, the Prince, I have the Russian film he loved so much." Chibisov pulled the reel of the movie *Chapayev* out of his carry bag and handed it to Gagarin.

Then he presented a can of Russian beer to Chernack. "If you do not make it as American Commander, you can always deliver beer in Russia."

Dinner and presentations over, the men retired to the bar for more toasts. Salnikov smiled. "Tonight, the good stuff," he said, and then he and Tiertsiev produced three bottles of Smirnoff vodka with Russian labels and stamps.

Privately, Chibisov pulled a casual picture of himself and his men on the hill with Gagarin out of a folder. He gave a copy each to Chernack and Gagarin. Both men would keep that photograph for the rest of their lives.

Chibisov, Gagarin, and the Soviet gang of four

Chapter 30

Yakutat to Yakutsk

Zebras make an unscheduled stop

Summer 1945. Project Zebra was coming to a close. The last 25 Nomads had come off the production lines in Philadelphia and been ferried to Elizabeth City. The plan was for one last group of American pilots to fly the planes to Anchorage, Alaska, where the Russians would take title and travel to Yakutsk, Siberia.

The American crews were given the freedom to make refueling stops where they saw fit because, as some of them explained to Chernack, they had families along the "approximate route."

Chernack knew "families" probably included girlfriends, sightseeing, and such, but as the war was winding down, so he rationalized that a "few extra stops at this point won't change the course of the war." The planes left Elizabeth City hours apart, traveling in squadrons of five. Gagarin and Chernack were part of the last squadron. The agreement was to meet at the Naval Air Base in Seattle and fly all 25 planes to Anchorage, again making refueling stops as weather permitted.[64] Because of the previously discussed Stalin-Roosevelt mutual no-fly rules, the final Russian crews — including Commander Chibisov — were flown directly to Elmendorf Airbase in Anchorage by American crews on US Navy DC-4s. They arrived in Anchorage days before the American Zebras.

Soviet Zebras at Elmendorf await their Nomads

Texas Air Force

Gagarin and Chernack were part of the final squadron of five planes that flew from Elizabeth City to Anchorage. There was no actual flight plan; stops were based on weather conditions and fuel consumption. Along the way, the planes landed at an Army base in Austin, Texas, to refuel before heading north to Seattle. They landed in Texas without incident. As they disembarked, they were surrounded by a bevy of curious maintenance crews and military officers.

The mechanics had never seen a plane that large, so they asked the crew for an onboard tour. The Texas Air Force officers had a different question because they'd never seen an amphibious plane with big red stars.

"Sir," said one of the officers, "never seen one of these. What's the red star?"

---

[64] Peak Nomad flying altitude was 12,000-14,000 feet, so they couldn't fly above most inclement weather conditions.

Gagarin's Texas Air Force arrives in Austin

Gagarin wasn't certain how to respond. Chernack winked at Gagarin, as if to say, "Let me take this one."

"Guess you boys haven't heard," said Chernack. "These planes are going to be part of the new Texas Air Force. The Navy is just doing test flights before delivery."

"That's one big plane," commented one of the mechanics.

"Texas is one big state," responded Chernack.

"Soldier," said Chernack, "It's important you don't tell anybody about what you've seen. Our mission is strictly top secret."

"Understand, *sir*. You can count on us, *sir*. Mum's the word," barked the mechanic.

Wandering Pilots

Even though Chernack's squad was last to leave, they arrived first in Seattle. Twelve hours went by, then 24, then 36. "Wonder if they ran into problems?" worried Chernack.

The planes began to arrive one by one at different times and from different directions. After a few questions, Chernack determined that this last group of pilots had decided, since the war was winding down, they might as well visit family and friends along the way. In fact, their log books indicated stops in New Orleans, Miami, Chicago, Omaha, and about a half dozen other places.

So much time had passed that Chernack ordered them to leave immediately and "take the most direct route, because the Soviets were probably already waiting in Anchorage."

Kodiak Island

The original plan was for Chernack's team to follow the next day, after he treated his crew to a nice dinner. By the time they left, however, weather conditions had changed. Strong headwinds forced them to land and refuel at an Army base in Kodiak, Alaska, which was now operating on a skeleton staff. As it turned out, the plane also required some maintenance that would necessitate an overnight stay on the base.

"Anything to do around here?" asked one of the crew.

The response surprised everybody. "Some of the best sightseeing." The men looked around; there were only a few gravel roads that headed into the wilderness. "Best way to get around these parts is by train-jeep." The men walked to the other side of the hangar. There they found a strange-looking jeep with steel wheels, sitting on a narrow, two-gauge railroad track. "These were made during the war. Just start driving, and you can go around parts of the island. Not sure how far; think the boys built about 50 or 60 miles. Takes you out to the harbor and back."

Boys tour the Kodiak countryside in their train-jeep

"Nobody will ever believe this," said Gagarin. So the men took pictures for their scrapbooks, and then spent the rest of the day learning why Kodiak is called "America's Emerald Isle." [65]

Steelheads Win

The next day, the Zebras had to make an important decision: travel about 600 miles to Anchorage, or take a 1,500-mile detour to Yakutat, Alaska, noted for the greatest salmon runs in the United States. Gagarin radioed the Anchorage base. According to the operator, the other American crews had already arrived, and Commander Chibisov and his team were busy preparing for their final departure to Siberia.

Chernack and Gagarin agreed. Next stop: Yakutat. From stories past, battling a 10-to-20-pound wild steelhead salmon was all but guaranteed to those who dropped their fishing lures into the pristine, crystal clear waters of the Situk River. [66]

The men arrived late in the day, had a nice dinner and a few drinks, and then went to bed. In the morning, they headed for the salmon streams. There they met a teenage Eskimo guide who rented his services along with some rudimentary fishing equipment. Chernack, an avid New England fisherman, couldn't believe his eyes. The salmon were running; you could almost touch the shiny Steelheads as they bounced in the river. The men rented the equipment — and the guide, for safe measure.

They handed the kid a five dollar bill. He waved the men off. Gagarin tried to explain they were only there for the day. The teen looked at his watch and pointed. It was 10:00 A.M.

"So?" wondered Gagarin.

"So it is too late. The fish have already eaten. You must get here much earlier."

---

[65] Kodiak is America's second largest island, and is noted for its fishing and forests. See References.

[66] Yakutat hosts the largest wild salmon population in Alaska. See References.

Chernack was determined and confident. "Nice, kid, but I've been fishing for decades. Just rent the boat and equipment." Four hours later, they didn't have so much as a nibble. Gagarin just smiled.

"How was I supposed to know about Alaskan salmon? We fish for Cod and Haddock on the Cape."

Oilpialluk's Guarantee

As the disappointed anglers returned to the base, four other Zebra officers stood there with a small Eskimo man. "Say hello to our guide, Oikpialluk."[67] Gagarin and Chernack were skeptical, but the others officers persisted. "Guys, what have we got to lose? Oikpialluk told us, 'No catch, no cost.'"

The crew of six followed Oikpialluk into the nearby woods, military-issue rifles in hand. They talked as they walked. After about an hour, the guide signaled "silence" by placing his hand over his mouth. The men waited patiently. The guide pointed. In the distance, two beautiful furry red wolves appeared in a small clearing. The guide aimed his gun and motioned to the others. They all aimed and shot, more or less simultaneously. One wolf fell to the ground; the other disappeared into the woods.

Oikpialluk made good on his guarantee. He split the wolf's carcass and hung it on a sturdy tree limb. The men carried their trophy back to the base and took a photo to record the event for posterity.

---

[67] In the Inuit culture, Oikpialluk means a "Man who can do so much for others." See References.

Oikpialluk and the happy Zebras show their trophy

When they were done taking pictures, the Zebras handed the guide the agreed ten-dollar fee. Gagarin was curious. "Who shot the wolf?"

The guide answered philosophically, "Does it matter?"

Chapter 31

Russians Do Anchorage

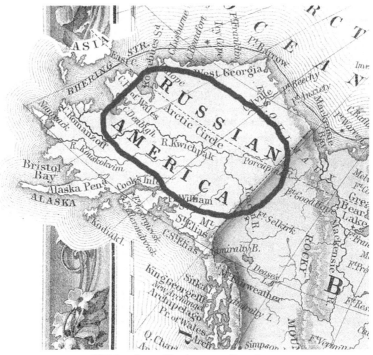

1856: when Alaska was Russian

As almost all American schoolchildren know, Secretary of State William Seward agreed to buy the land mass we know as Alaska from the Russian Government in 1867 for 7.2 million dollars.

That purchase effectively ended Russian efforts to expand trade and settlements to the Pacific coast of North America. It was also an important step in the United States' rise as a great Pacific power.

For three decades after the purchase, the US paid little attention to Alaska, which was governed by military, naval, or treasury rule or, at times, no visible rule at all. Skeptics had dubbed the purchase of

Alaska "Seward's Folly," [68] but the former Secretary was vindicated when gold was discovered in the Yukon in 1896. Alaska quickly became the gateway to the Klondike gold fields.

The military importance of Alaska was finally recognized during World War II. The construction of the Alaska-Canada Military Highway, a 1,420-mile wilderness road, was completed in less than nine months. Then telephone lines, oil pipelines, railways, and roughly 300 military bases were installed throughout Alaska.

A Fish Story

Russians have always had a love affair with sport fishing, partially because of their geography: Russia occupies one-eighth of the world's land mass and contains two million rivers, which contain more than 80 percent of all freshwater species, particularly wild salmon.[69] Not surprisingly, Chibisov was a skilled freshwater fisherman.

Chibisov searches for Alaskan Steelheads

[68] Purchasing Alaska. See References.

[69] For more on fish species and rivers see references.

Chibisov and his crew grew impatient waiting for Chernack, Gagarin, and their crew to arrive at Elmendorf Air Base. Chibisov decided to do a little fishing for the famed Alaskan Steelhead. Despite struggling with speaking English, he obtained a jeep and a topographical map, which indicated a salmon-rich river, the Kenai, within a day's driving distance. When he and a few crew members arrived at the river, they found a rowboat, some rudimentary fishing tackle, and an old Eskimo guide, who could barely speak English, much less Russian. Half an hour and five dollars later, Chibisov rowed toward the middle of the calm waters, while the others took their coats off and fell fast asleep on the sunny shore. In a while, there was a strong tug on Chibisov's line, and soon he had bagged a 12-pound steelhead. On shore, one of the men happened to have a camera, and he took a picture of their Commander and his catch. Another pointed to the large body of fresh water and said, "Like Baikal. No?" [70]

Chibisov smiled. "Very good but no Baikal."

Commander Max proudly displays his prized catch

---

[70] Lake Baikal is the largest freshwater lake in the world. It covers 9,000 square meters, with a depth of 5,400 feet at its deepest point. See References.

Confused and Bewildered

The planes arrived and all the men met up. According to the mechanics, it would take five or six days to thoroughly check and get the 25 Nomads ready for their 2,500-mile trip across northern Alaska and on to Yakutsk, Siberia.

"Why so long?' asked Gagarin.

"The war is winding down, sir; we are not at full staff. Besides, it's going to take a day to load the spare parts, assuming we can find room among all those other boxes."

Gagarin looked at Chibisov. They spoke in Russian so no one else would understand. Chibisov insisted, "This time not too heavy. I double checked myself."

The men spent time seeing the sites. As Chibisov explained, he would like to see Russia's America, referring to the Seward purchase. Their first stop was a 100-year old Eastern Orthodox Church. A cemetery around back had graves marked with the three-bar Orthodox cross. Chibisov asked, "How long ago did America buy?" When Gagarin told him it was 80 years ago, Chibisov simply repeated, "Eighty years!"

Eastern Orthodox Church built around 1900

Next stop was the main drag, Fourth Street in downtown. That, too, was not what Chibisov expected. There were lots of late-model automobiles, stores, restaurants, and smiling people. He also noticed that the bookstores sold classic Russian literature in Russian.

Circa 1940s Anchorage taking shape as a bustling city

Chibisov discovered that, despite the land having been sold to America, many Russians had stayed and were now Russian-Americans. As they walked to the bustling harbor, he saw fisherman loading cargo boats with mountains of freshly caught fish, while boxes of fruits and vegetables were being unloaded.

Chibisov shook his head. "I don't understand why Russia sold Alaska to Americans. I think you robbed; price much too low." There wasn't much Gagarin could say; the resource-rich Alaska was indeed a steal.

Emotional Farewell

In a few days, the planes were ready to leave. The Zebra officers on both sides knew their 18-month journey was something none of them would ever forget. They had learned about one others' culture; they had learned to laugh and work together as brothers; they had learned to trust and depend on one other. To these men, what they would read, see, and hear for the rest of their lives would be judged against what they had experienced during their time together.

03 Sept 45. Chibisov gives orders to the final Soviet crews

Chibisov was the last man to board. He stood alone on the tarmac next to Gagarin. The men shook hands. "Thank you for all that you have done. I will never forget," said the hearty Chibisov with a tear running down his cheek.

He took his treasured Red Army wings off the front of his coat and handed them to Gagarin. "I hope you will remember me when you look at these."

Chibisov's wings, long-treasured by Gagarin

Gagarin responded simply, "We will meet again." As it happened, they never did.

Chapter 32

Soviet Zebras at Home

Soviet Commander Ivanov and pilots Yakovlev, Levtchishin,
and Dyatchenko arrive in Yakutsk, Siberia

Coming home meant serious adjustments for Chibisov. He had left a place where "life's little things so easy to accomplish" and returned to a world dominated by an angry, determined Stalin.

Despite the immense military and civilian sacrifices, Stalin was furious that the USSR had been rebuffed as a trustworthy ally and not included in the newly formed North Atlantic Treaty Organization alliance. That rejection boomeranged. Stalin became consumed by two goals: to become a feared military power that would not be deterred by anyone or any group of countries, and to show the world that a government-controlled communist state with definitive Five-Year Plans could compete economically with the West.

He achieved his military goal, but failed on the economic front. Despite the obvious difficulties of everyday life, Stalin's absolute control over postwar Soviet propaganda machines made the terrible seem terrific. He carefully cultivated his image as "Uncle Joe," the kind, homely man who was the father of all Russians. Posters featured him surrounded by adoring children. Those who attempted to listen, read, or discuss otherwise were severely punished. Everybody knew of the labor camps, and that was enough of a deterrent. [71]

Uncle Joe's carefully cultivated image

Soviet Zebras

Stories of bravery and patriotism in the Great Patriotic War were featured in books, movies, and newspapers, and quickly became part of every classroom curriculum. But the Project Zebra mission was little known and never publicly celebrated in either the USSR or the Russian Federation.

Stalin knew Zebra had been a significant combat success, but he wanted to minimize the credit given to the capitalist West for any Soviet military successes. In fact, Stalin spoke of the entire Lend-

---

[71] Life in the USSR under Stalin. See References.

Lease program as a "relatively insignificant military program that helped shorten the war by just a few months."

Circa 1960. Major-General Maxim Chibisov

All this left Chibisov in a difficult position. He and his Zebras had learned firsthand that Western society's values and economic wealth were not quite as Stalin portrayed it. But he was also committed to remaining a respected senior member of the military, because it boded well for him and his family. So Chibisov said nothing, and, in time, Maxim's military skills were rewarded with the rank of major-general.

Things began to change after Stalin's death. There was a growing curiosity about Project Zebra, the military mission that seemed lost in time. The military was curious because it was the only Stalin-approved military mission ever conducted on American soil. Since the mission remained top secret in America, there were no official reports and no press accounts, just bits and pieces shared by word-of-mouth through the Soviet's mission expert, Maxim Chibisov.

Periodically, Maxim even received approval to organize a gathering where some of the Zebras would meet, reminisce, and take photos for themselves, their families, and for posterity, without fear of reprisal.

Soviet Zebras post-war gathering in Moscow

Despite the growing interest in Project Zebra, anti-US sentiment remained high during the Khrushchev and Brezhnev years. Consequently, Chibisov's formal presentations and informal conversations focused exclusively on the military aspects of the mission: the enormous planes designed with Soviet assistance, the dangerous return routes for Zebra crews, and the Nomads' many uses created by Soviet ingenuity. He felt that revealing the personal side of Zebra would either be considered an exaggeration or, worse yet, treason.

Maxim explains the Zebra mission to the Soviet press

The Diaries

Privately, however, Chibisov revealed to family and friends many of the observations made in his diaries. He told them of the America he had come to know, including his moments of personal challenge and incidents of good humor.

He spoke glowingly to his daughters, Emilia and Yelena, of the American with Russian blood, Prince Grigorievich Gagarin, "the man who had helped your father live both worlds." The girls never forgot their father's words about America and about the people of Elizabeth City. His daughters hoped to one day visit the site of Project Zebra.

A Lucky Man

Besides his career and his country, Chibisov had one other passion — his family. His wife, Rozochka, predeceased him in 1983, leaving him with two daughters who admired him and three grandchildren who adored him.

Circa 1985. Grandpa Max surrounded by his daughters,
Yelena and Emilia, and his three grandchildren.

He wrote in his diary, shortly before his death in 1986 at the age of 75, "I consider myself a lucky man. I have had everything one may desire – the job I liked so much, good friends, two wonderful daughters, and my life partner, my 'guardian angel,' beloved Rozochka.

"I flew for 37 years without emergencies. I survived in the heavy fire on numerous occasions during the Second World War because I was guarded by my little star. In our life together, Rozochka went through much pain and suffering. She was told twice that I was dead, but she didn't believe that. She just prayed and waited. Soon after both occasions, I emerged unscathed from any troublesome and dangerous situations."[72]

---

[72] The Bliss of Flying. See References.

At his eulogy, one of Chibisov's colleagues said, "This is a man all Russians can take pride in. He was that kind of a person. But above all, he was a soldier, always willing to serve his Homeland."

Lost in Time

During the remainder of his military career, Maxim Chibisov received more awards and honors than 99 percent of the other Russian officers that served during WWII. Despite those accomplishments, Maxim Chibisov's name is practically unknown today in Russia, and completely unknown in the rest of the world. As you will read in the final chapter, activities are underway to change this.

A lifetime of service, awards, and honors

Prized Possession

Of all the memorabilia Maxim Chibisov collected during his military career, a letter dated October 3, 1945, from US Navy Vice Admiral Paul Bellinger held a special place. It read in part:

"The U.S. Naval personnel who worked with [the men of the Soviet Union] have nothing but the highest praise for the excellence, competence, and cooperative spirit of the officers and men of your country who have come to America....

239

"I am sure... the spirit of cooperation and understanding between our two great countries that has grown from such contacts as this will continue to the mutual benefit of each."

Chibisov's US peer, Commander Chernack, was copied on Bellinger's correspondence. Although Chibisov and Chernack never spoke again, Chernack stored his letter among his treasured Project Zebra papers, which remained sealed until 2017.

3 October 1945

My dear Captain Skriagin:

As the project for transferring Catalina aircraft from the United States to the Soviet Union nears completion, may I take the opportunity to express to you my very high regard for the Russian airmen who participated in the project -- pilots, navigators, engineers, and radiomen alike.

The U. S. Naval personnel who worked with them have nothing but the highest praise for the excellence, competence, and cooperative spirit of the officers and men of your country who have come to America, worked in complete harmony with our people, and flown the Catalinas to Russia in all seasons and under all weather conditions. Cooperating with them in the common effort that led to the defeat of Germany and Japan has been a pleasant and stimulating experience.

May I mention, in particular, that my own association with Colonel M. N. Chibisov, Commander of the Detachment, and Lieutenant Colonel V. A. Tertsiev, Chief Technical advisor, has been thoroughly enjoyable. I have great personal esteem for both officers.

I am sure that the fine spirit of cooperation and understanding between our two great countries that has grown from such contacts as this will continue to the mutual benefit of each.

Very sincerely yours,

P.N.L. BELLINGER,
Vice Admiral, U. S. Navy.

Captain N. A. Skriagin
Acting Naval Attache, Navy of the U.S.S.R.
2234 Massachusetts, Avene
Washington, D. C.

Copy to:
Lt.Cdr. S.I.Chernak, U.S.N.R.

Vice Admiral Bellinger's letter of praise for Soviet Zebras

Accidental Observation

When one writes a book such as *Project Zebra*, they sometimes come upon an accidental, but relevant, observation. As I researched and collected pictures from all over the world, I realized that, even though there was a Cold War after Project Zebra, the Russian Zebras remained proud of what they had accomplished and sought each other's company.

In the following montage, you will see a post-war   Zebra gathering, perhaps from the early 1960s. Two of those officers visited the Wright Brothers at Kitty Hawk and then went fishing with Colonel Chibisov in Alaska. And Maxim kept his word; he never forgot his experience in America with the Americans. Apparently, he also did everything in his power to make sure the men who reported to him did the same, despite the Cold War, Stalin, and the never-ending barrage of misinformation between our two nations.

Chapter 33

American Zebras at Home

Senator Joseph McCarthy's paranoia runs rampant

The years after WWII were filled with pride, optimism, and prosperity. The media told us we saved the world, and we believed it. Our natural wealth, geographic isolation, and entrepreneurial spirit were revered and envied around the world.

The fiercely anti-Soviet Harry Truman took office in 1945, after the premature death of Franklin Roosevelt, who had just begun to engender some long-term goodwill with Stalin at the Yalta Conference.

The domestically-minded Truman knew little of the talks and seemed to have little interest in the results. Just a few years earlier as a Senator, he had said publicly, "If we see that Germany is winning, we ought to help Russia, and if Russia is winning, we ought to help Germany, and that way let them kill as many as possible."

Nothing changed when he became President. Truman was suspicious of every communist move. Truman attended the Potsdam Conference, which was to deal with a vision for post-war Germany. Irreconcilable differences emerged immediately. Truman saw a reconstructed Germany as prosperous, Western-style democracy, and a trading partner. Stalin was appalled by that idea. Given the huge loss of life and the damage done to Russian infrastructure, Stalin wanted the German machine humbled, and reparations paid. He also wanted a geographic buffer built around Germany so that Russia could never again be invaded.

Truman and Stalin: distrust flourishes[73]

Like Churchill, Truman believed Stalin was a "devil-like tyrant leading a vile system." He saw Stalin's actions in Eastern Europe as a dictator's "aggressive expansionism, completely incompatible with the agreements Stalin agreed to at Yalta just the previous year."

---

[73] Artist Bob Row, 1947. See References.

Despite their differences, Truman and Stalin put on a good show, drinking toasts to everyone and posing for photographs. Truman even declared, "I can deal with Comrade Stalin. He is honest but smart as hell." Privately, Truman sang another tune. "The Russians only understand one language — how many armies have you got?"

Stalin never showed his hand publicly, but left Potsdam even more convinced that America would use its economic advantages and success to entice other nations to expand their capitalist leanings.

The Potsdam Conference was the first and only time Truman would ever meet Stalin in person. Most historians would suggest Potsdam was the unofficial beginning of the Cold War. [74]

Truman's strong and growing anti-Soviet beliefs, and the detailed reporting of such by the press, led many ordinary citizens to believe that the prospect of communist subversion, both at home and abroad, was frighteningly real. For many Americans, the most enduring symbol of this "Red Scare" was Republican Senator Joseph P. McCarthy of Wisconsin. Senator McCarthy spent almost five years trying in vain to expose communists and other left-wing "loyalty risks" in the US government. In the hyper-suspicious atmosphere of the Cold War, insinuations of disloyalty were enough to convince some Americans that their government was packed with traitors and spies. McCarthy's accusations were so intimidating that few people dared to speak out against him. It was not until he attacked the Army in 1954 that his actions earned him the censure of the US Senate.

American Zebra Story

Against this backdrop, Project Zebra remained top secret, so there was little media coverage of the historic partnership. On September 26, 1946, 12 months after the final Nomad left Elizabeth City,[75] only two national stories ever appeared in the mainstream news media. The popular *New York Journal-American* ran a front-

[74] Impressions of Truman and Stalin. See References.

[75] For entire NYT and NY Sun story, see References.

page story about Project Zebra in which they properly labeled Zebra a pet project of President Roosevelt.

*Journal-American story based on what
was known at the time*

A day later, the *New York Times* ran essentially the same story, with some additional incorrect facts relating to how many planes there were and how many Soviets were trained.

Soviet Received 100 U.S. Seaplanes Equipped With Bombsights, Radar

By The United Press.

WASHINGTON, Sept. 26—The Navy disclosed today that it secretly trained 140 Russian airmen in this country in 1944 as part of a $100,000, in which 188 N 100 of them Norden bombs types of radio and radar gear, were transferred to Russia.

The Navy gave no details on the agreement, but it was reported that the project received a high priority

ered in 1945. "Operation Zebra" was ended last Oct. 20. and he estimated that the lend-lease agreement for the planes totaled 0.

count of the proj- ed in a historical Air Wing Five, which conducted the operation.

The first group of sixty Russian airmen reported to the Elizabeth City, N. C., naval air station, April 3. 1944. Eighty more arrived there

The New York Times
Published: September 27, 1946

New York Times publishes a derivative version of the Zebra story

The subsequent Cold War frenzy ensured that the mission would be classified as top-secret for another 68 years, and there would be no subsequent news stories about it published by any major news organization.

Virtually no ranking American officer or historian seems to have ever heard of Project Zebra. This is strange, given that fact that this was the only time in history that Russian flying aces were trained in the continental United States. They were here for 18-24 months to fly 158 American-made, technically-advanced amphibious aircraft the size of today's 737 jetliners. The lengthy declassification process of the project may simply have been an oversight. But given all the other secret missions that have been made public, one might hypothesize that American officials — like Stalin and his counterparts — simply wanted the phenomenon of postwar enemies working so closely together to disappear into the myths of history.

Keeping in Touch

On the American side, only Gagarin and Chernack kept in touch, although they would only meet in person twice during the next 50 years.

The first was at a lounge in New York City. The two men had a few drinks, reminisced about good old Zebra days, and expressed their chagrin that they could do nothing about Cold War anti-American sentiment. "Talking favorably about our Soviet colleagues at that moment would be like siding with today's radical Islamic terrorists," said Gagarin.

One story they recalled was "The Elizabeth City Hurricane Miscalculation."

The Outer Banks and environs were susceptible to hurricanes. The weather forecast indicated a Category 3 hurricane that would be hitting the mainland in several hours, with winds estimated at 110 to 130 mph. The Naval Base Headquarters Squad 5 maintenance staff spent hours securing the Soviet Nomads to sturdy grommets installed on the tarmac for just such a contingency. The rear of each plane faced the Pasquotank River, at the edge of the base.

Gagarin looked in the direction of the oncoming breeze and the angry gray sky. He said something to Chernack, who replied simply, "So tell them."

Gagarin knew Squad 5 was not under the command of the Zebra mission, so he approached the subject tactfully. He explained that the wind at the eye of the storm looked like it going to come up the river.

Gagarin suggested that it might be better if the nose of the planes pointed in the direction of the wind, as they would when flying into stormy weather at sea. The officer looked around. Virtually all the planes were secured, and he was not about to redo the grommets.

"Respectfully, sir, we're good. The Soviet planes are well secured," the officer said.

Gagarin replied that they were still our planes. The Soviets didn't take title until the last leg. "If the storm damages them, it will be up to you to fix. Do we understand each other?"

Again, the officer replied, "Like I said, sir, we're good to go."

Two hours later, Soviet and American Zebras sat together in Zebra World Headquarters drinking coffee and talking when the storm hit. Rattling and clanking noises came from the tarmac. The men looked out the window as plane after plane tore free of the grommets and smashed into one another.

Then the eye of the storm passed and the sun appeared. The runway was a mess. Gagarin stared. The Navy maintenance officer stared. Nobody said anything. Repairs took about a week, so the Soviet Zebras had some unexpected free time. They used it productively; they did some last-minute shopping in Elizabeth City, had drinks at the Virginia Dare Bar, and ate a few meals downtown.

Fifty Years Later
December 2007. Gagarin had been told by Chernack's son Peter that his father, now 93, was failing for no reason other than old age. Out of respect, Gagarin decided to visit Chernack at the hospital.

"He looked so thin. He wasn't the Stanley I knew. I recalled a few of our Narragansett excursions to visit his wife and kids. I mentioned how he called the Island as a good place to hide out with a Navy plane on weekends. Stanley reached for my hand. He smiled fondly, 'I remember, Lieutenant.' We said our goodbyes, and as I left, I felt a tear roll down my cheek.

"The next day I received a call from his son Peter, who said, 'Dad died a few hours ago. I just thought you'd want to know. Other than family, you were the last person to see him.'"

Chapter 34

Collateral Damage

Harry S Truman took office on April 12, 1945. From that moment forward, Truman's open disdain for Stalin and all things Russian set the stage for the Cold War. It also created a piece of collateral damage that exists to this day. The efforts of the ten Navy officers who managed Project Zebra from start to finish — including Chernack and Gagarin — were simply placed in the dust bin of history.

Unexpected Recognition

Chibisov sensed the growing rancor at home and on the world stage. Despite these realities, he felt the results of Project Zebra had exceeded all of his and his country's expectations. He wanted the American chain of command to know that, even at the risk of incurring the wrath of Stalin.

US Navy Vice Admiral Paul Bellinger

On September 15, 1945, the US Naval Commander, Vice Admiral Paul Bellinger, received a letter, delivered by a messenger from the Russian Embassy in Washington, D.C. It read in part:

"The assignment given to me by my government — the ferrying to the Soviet Union of the Catalina planes so graciously granted to us by your Government...

"...My profound apologies for daring to write to you personally, considering the difference in our positions and ranks, but believe me, Admiral, I cannot leave your country where I was greeted so warmly without having expressed my deep feeling [sic] of gratitude and appreciation to you, one of the most respected officers of your country and one who has so carefully and attentively regarded our requests and needs...

"I am taking the liberty of asking you to thank and honor all the officers and men... who helped accomplish this task. And, I especially wish to distinguish Lt. Commander Chernack who has so energetically and fruitfully contributed to the proficient fulfillment of this assignment...

"I shall take the greatest pleasure in telling the people of my country about the warm and friendly reception accorded me and my officers during our stay... The deep feeling of esteem and appreciation for you will remain with me forever."

My Dear Admiral Bellinger:

    The assignment given to me by my Government – the ferrying to the Soviet Union of the Catalina planes so graciously granted to us by your Government – is nearing an end.

    During the year and a half that this work has been in progress, we have successfully ferried 184 planes to the USSR. These planes were immediately put into action and thus contributed to the defeat of Germany and Japan.

    The successful fulfilment of my assignment is due to the colossal help rendered us by you personally and by the officers under your command.

    I wish to express my profound apologies for daring to write to you personally, considering the difference in our positions and ranks, but believe me, Admiral, I cannot leave your country where I was greeted so warmly without having expressed my deep feeling of gratitude and appreciation to you, one of the most respected officers of your country and one who has so carefully and attentively regarded our requests and needs.

    I am taking the liberty of asking you to thank and honor all the officers and men under your command who have helped us so immensely in accomplishing this task. I trust that this list of their names slights none.

    I wish to distinguish especially Lt. Comdr. Chernack who has so energetically and fruitfully contributed to the expeditious and proficient fulfilment of this assignment.

    In closing, Admiral, I wish to express my sincere and heartfelt hope that the spirit of mutual understanding and respect that has arisen between our people and their representatives will endure.

    I shall take the greatest pleasure in telling the people of my country about the warm and friendly reception accorded me and my officers during our stay at one of the bases under your jurisdiction. The deep feeling of esteem and appreciation for you will remain with me forever.

                     Very sincerely yours,

                      M. Chibisov
                      Colonel, USSR Air Forces

Maxim Chibisov's heartfelt and hopeful letter[76]

    Bellinger was impressed by Chibisov's initiative and recalled Colonel Tiertsiev's letter of appreciation to Commander Szekely of the Naval Aircraft Factory. It was clear to him that the American officers in charge of Project Zebra should be recognized for their professional and sensitive handling of one of the most extraordinary partnerships in military history.

---

[76] Archives of the Department of the Navy. See References.

In May 1946, Bellinger forwarded a recommendation to the Secretary of the Navy to award each American Zebra officer a Distinguished Service Medal of Honor. Supporting documentation included, among other papers: Colonel Chibisov's letter to Bellinger and Colonel Tiertsiev's letter of commendation to Naval Aircraft Factory Commander Szekely.

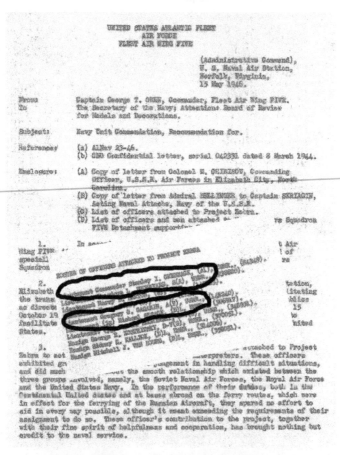

Bellinger directed award letter and officer list [77]

Seventy-one years later, as of 2017, the Secretary of the Navy has yet to respond.

---

[77] Archives of the Department of the Navy. See References.

Chapter 35

Return to Rodina

Gagarin was an aristocratic Russian name for centuries

Once a Russian, always a Russian. This is particularly true when your grandfather was the founder and first rector of the highly respected Polytechnic Institute in St. Petersburg. And when your great-grandfather was the primary artist in the court of Tsar Nicholas II.

Free Time

Despite his illustrious background, former US Navy Lieutenant Gagarin, now in his early 60s, had never actually set foot in Russia. Over the years, both pre- and post-Zebra, he stayed in touch with his cousins and family through letters and an occasional phone call. That changed in the late 1970s. At that time, Gagarin was a consultant for a company that licensed foundries to manufacture a patented shock absorber — The Draft Gear — for railroad car couplings. He found himself in Paris with three days of free time before his next appointment in England.

President Richard Nixon had just made history as the only American President to address the Russian people from the Kremlin on live television.

Circa 1972. President Nixon broadcasts from the Kremlin.

"Yesterday, I laid a wreath at the cemetery which commemorates the brave people who died during the siege of Leningrad in World War II," said Nixon. "At the cemetery, I saw the picture of a 12-year-old girl. She was a beautiful child. Her name was Tanya Savicheva. The pages of her diary tell the terrible story of war. In the simple words of a child, she wrote of the deaths of the members of her family: 'Zhenya in December. Grannie in January. Leka then next. Then Uncle Vasya. Then Uncle Lyosha. Then Mama. And then the Savichevs. All are dead. Only Tanya is left.'"

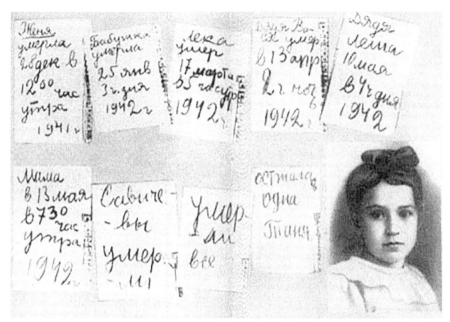

An important Soviet face of the Great Patriotic War

Nixon's final thought: "Our two great nations should never again allow another tragedy like Tanya."

Nixon's closing remarks deeply moved Gagarin. He called his cousin Tanya Gagarin in St. Petersburg to say he was in the general area. He learned that the Saint Petersburg Polytechnic Institute, the prestigious engineering school his grandfather had founded, was about to celebrate its 75th anniversary. The next day, thanks to his fluent French and Russian heritage, he was on a short flight to St. Petersburg with a visa in hand.

Upon arrival, he was met by a delegation of Gagarins he had never met: cousins, nieces, aunts, and uncles. "They all began kissing in the Russian way: three times on the cheek — left, right, left," recalled Gagarin. "The joy was overwhelming."

That first evening, they had a family feast at Tanya's. They drank vodka with bread and cheese, vodka with smoked salmon, and vodka with pickled herring and cucumbers. "The more we ate and drank, the more food and drinks appeared," smiled Gagarin.

Gagarin and his Russian relatives in Moscow

Visiting Grandpa

The next day, Gagarin and a few of his relatives traveled by train to the Polytechnic Institute in St. Petersburg, where a tour of the school had been arranged. There he learned that the Institute, considered the most advanced engineering school in Russia, was modeled after his alma mater, M.I.T.

Rector Gagarin (with paper) and his academic colleagues

The Institute had a sprawling campus, grand lecture halls, and 16 different schools structured around four primary departments: economics, electro-mechanics, metallurgy, and aviation & aerodynamics. The campus also housed numerous scientific research laboratories, and 20,000 undergraduate and doctorate students. About 50 percent of the members of prestigious Russia Academy of Sciences were graduates of the school. [78]

Polytechnic campus during Gagarin's visit

During the tour, Gagarin saw the bust of his grandfather prominently placed in the entry hall, sat in on a few classes, and had lunch with faculty members. During that luncheon, the Institute Director asked if Gagarin would like to share a few comments with interested students. He agreed. Gagarin addressed hundreds of students and faculty members in a large lecture hall. "When word of your return to Rodina spread, everyone wanted to be here," said the director.

The bulletin board behind the lecture stand was filled with artifacts from World War II. Gagarin wondered if they had come to learn some details of Project Zebra. The questions that ensued suggested no. Those in attendance were more interested in the personal journey

---

[78] The Polytechnic Institute. See References.

of the only Russian Prince ever to become an American officer in the service of the United States.

After the extensive Q&A session, which included a question or two regarding his father's daring escape from the Bolsheviks, Gagarin made some heartfelt remarks. He complimented the students on attending such a noted academic institution because he believed, as an MIT graduate, that "science and technology" would be important tools for future generations. He also thanked the faculty for running the university so effectively. "My grandfather would be proud of your legacy."

Circa 1974. Gagarin speaks at the Polytechnic Institute

Other Impressions

The visit to the motherland brought other observations. Some were new, others assumed.

Everything in the city seemed to work, but nothing was quite up to current standards in most developed countries. "It was as if the world had grown up faster than Stalin and his system could improve things," said Gagarin.

As he walked around St. Petersburg, Gagarin also noticed very few traffic signs relative to the volume of traffic, and that the roadways needed a lot of work. "You wouldn't want to drive a new car over those potholes."

As he stopped for coffee, he got the impression that many ordinary citizens were aware of some of these shortcomings — perhaps because returning soldiers told of what they had seen elsewhere, or perhaps because travel was no longer restricted and they had been personally exposed to how other social democracies lived.

When he visited his cousin Tanya's apartment, he realized his family was, as Chibisov might have said, a "real Russian." His family knew how to find humor in everyday difficulties.

Tanya's modest apartment entryway had chipped paint and was dimly lit, with litter randomly piled behind the steps. The elevator to Tanya's fourth-floor apartment didn't work. Gagarin saw a small yellow sign near the elevator which said, "under repair." He asked his cousin when the work was expected to be completed. She laughed. "The repairs will be done when the government gets around to it, unless you are willing to pay extra rubles to get to the top of the list."

She added that this was not possible at the moment. This past month, the family had used their extra rubles to buy gasoline for a family trip and to pay the police for an imaginary traffic violation.

Before leaving St. Petersburg, Gagarin promised his relatives that he would one day return with his wife and daughter Katherine. "All the Gagarins should understand their roots."

Plane Ride Back

Gagarin was happy he had taken the Rodina detour. As he opened the newspaper, the lead story spoke of "our prince's return."

Thoughts then turned to his father. Would he have enjoyed seeing the family again? Did he realize the impact of the Polytechnic achievements? Would he ever return to the Homeland to visit his own father? They were questions Gagarin couldn't answer as he recalled a childhood without a father. He recalled a childhood in which he was raised by his grandparents — his mother, Elizabeth, had become the family breadwinner because his father had gone to America to find a better life.

When Gregory was 12 years old, his mother received a letter from his father inviting Gregory to spend the summer of 1934 at his riding academy in Long Island. Young Gregory traveled five days across the Atlantic by himself, not even knowing what his father would look like when he arrived. Despite all of that, the two had a great summer together at the riding school. At the end of that fun-filled summer, Gregory realized for the first time how much he missed having a father. As he boarded the boat to go back to Paris, his father asked if he'd like to come back the next summer. Greg replied, "Why not invite Mother, too?"

Mom and Dad in America after a long separation

"Do you think she would come?" asked his father.

"I don't know why not," replied Gregory.

The following year, the Gagarins were reunited in America and lived happily ever after.

Chapter 36

Ann's Glasnost

Too much, too soon?

The Soviet Union operated as a centrally-planned economy for almost 70 years. Most of the structure originated under Stalin, with only slight modifications during the Khrushchev and Brezhnev eras.

This central planning system allowed Soviet leaders to marshal resources in times of crisis, and to turn the Soviet Union into a postwar military superpower. However, the country's overall economic growth lagged far behind the market-based economy of its capitalist adversary, the United States.

GDPpc growth

<u>U.S.S.R. versus United States</u>

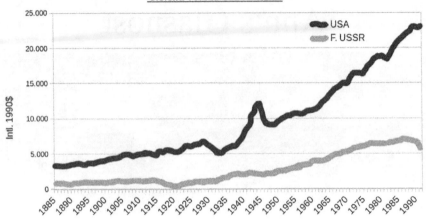

USSR per capita growth lagged post-WWII

Enter Mikhail Gorbachev

After the untimely death of the more traditional Konstantin Chernenko in 1985, the younger, pro-West leaning Mikhail Gorbachev was elected General Secretary of the Communist Party. In a short period, he had befriended President Ronald Reagan, dismantled the Communist infrastructure, dissolved the USSR, and introduced his new system of economic reform, called *Perestroika*. Under his modified system of socialism, enterprise managers were to be given control over contracts and operations, and they were to introduce certain aspects of a free market economy. Gorbachev wanted to make enterprise managers responsible for making a profit.

Gorbachev also believed these new economic reforms would be more successful in an atmosphere where issues could be discussed and resolved openly. This focus on human values, instead of historical class struggles, was called *Glasnost*[79] (openness).

After a brief period of citizen euphoria, deep-seated resistance developed on several fronts: the privileged felt threatened;

---

[79] Glasnost, a new openness, and Perestroika, new economic reform, were supposed to be hallmarks of the New Russian Federation.

organizational infrastructures were scaled for socialist beliefs, not capitalist efficiencies; and the common worker, accustomed to predictive roles and responsibilities, became disoriented. In short, Gorbachev's ideas were too much, too soon. While a small amount of private enterprise emerged, the general population resented the profiteering, particularly since they now had to pay four or five times more for certain goods due to shortages and corruption. In the end, nobody knew how to make a capitalist profit while still providing the long-standing basic social benefits. Perestroika was repealed on August 28, 1990, and Gorbachev resigned [80] a short time later.

В ЦКК КПСС

РЕЗОЛЮЦИЯ

3-я Всесоюзной конференции общества "Единство, за ленинизм и коммунистические идеалы, 28 октября 1990 г., г.Ленинград

О ПОЛИТИЧЕСКОМ НЕДОВЕРИИ

ГЕНЕРАЛЬНОМУ СЕКРЕТАРЮ ЦК КПСС М.С.ГОРБАЧЕВУ

Перед лицом катастрофических для народа, страны и партии последствий проводимой по инициативе М.С.Горбачева политики так называемой "перестройки", ввиду того, что этот курс совершенно определенно выявил свой буржуазно-реставраторский характер, и учитывая стоящую на пороге еще более тяжкую общенациональную катастрофу, в связи с планируемым введением в действие на территории страны стабилизационных программ" Международного валютного фонда, замаскированных под программы перехода к рыночной экономике, 3-я Всесоюзная конференция общества "Единство, за ленинизм и коммунистические идеалы",

выражает политическое недоверие М.С.Горбачеву, как Генеральному секретарю ЦК КПСС.

Мы считаем, что единственной силой в стране, способной изменить ход событий в конструктивном направлении, не доводя дело до гражданской войны, продолжает сегодня оставаться партия коммунистов.

Мы призываем всех честных, социалистически и патриотически настроенных членов КПСС, членов Центрального Комитета и ЦКК КПСС, партийные организации всех уровней, компартии союзных республик, потребовать созыва Чрезвычайного съезда КПСС, на котором поставить вопрос:

1. Об отстранении М.С.Горбачева и наиболее ревностных его сподвижников в развязывании буржуазной контрреволюции в СССР со всех выборных партийных постов и об исключении их из рядов Коммунистической партии Советского Союза.

2. Об отзыве М.С.Горбачева и названных лиц из депутатского

Gorbachev loses; Perestroika officially repealed

---

[80] Gorbachev and the Collapse of USSR. See References.

Against this backdrop, Greg Gagarin's wife, Ann, and his daughter Katherine, now 39, made their first trip to this new Russia. Gregory was anxious to expose his family to his heritage and spend time with the Chibisov family, who had written to Greg to tell him about their father's peaceful passing surrounded by family. In subsequent letters, he also learned of Chibisov's distinguished naval career, his promotion to Major-General, and the placement of a bronze bust of Chibisov in Moscow's prestigious Hall of Commanders.

Green Train

Despite this "new openness," there were still long delays in obtaining personal visas — even for former royal families like the Gagarins. So instead, they flew to Moscow with a scholastic tour group, and remained there with them for a few days while Gagarin himself finalized other trip details.

First stop was Holmby, to see the old family estate. The family traveled overnight in a communist-era dark green, coal-powered steel train from Moscow to St. Petersburg, accompanied by a group of excited aunts, uncles, and cousins they had never before met. From St. Petersburg, they would be driven by car to the city of Pskov, some 40 miles south.

The first person to enter the train was a handsome young man also named Gregory. He carried a big bouquet of flowers and a sign that read, "Welcome to Russia." The two Gregory's hugged. Suddenly, the train was flooded with Gagarins and baskets of food. One by one they kissed, hugged, and welcomed their three family visitors. "We eat while we travel," said Cousin Tanya.

Traveling in a numbered communist-era green train

Before Ann knew it, there was a huge spread of food on the train seat tables. (There were no food-service cars at that time. There was only a large Samovar with hot water, which you paid for by the cup. You were also expected to bring your own tea and cups.)

"I never saw such a huge assortment of food on a train before," said Ann. She recalled beet salads — chopped, sliced, and minced — numerous types of borscht; sandwiches made with fish and poultry; and some less familiar fare. "Taste," said one of the cousins, handing Ann what looked like a thin slice of white cheese on a square of black bread, "Salo; Russian delicacy."[81]

Ann ate it, then asked Greg what she had eaten. He told her, "Sliced, salted pork fat." That was the last unfamiliar item Ann would eat on the entire trip.

Ann also noticed that one of the cousins had a heavily bandaged right hand. The cousin had cut her hand badly while preparing the food feast the previous day, and blood was still seeping. "I thought to

---

[81] The Salo cult. See References.

myself, shouldn't this young lady be going to a doctor?" Another cousin arrived. She began mumbling something in Russian, running her hand over the damp bandage. A few minutes later, the blood stopped weeping, and the women re-bandaged her hand. "Jeez Louise," thought Ann, "What was that about??"

Body Odor

Gagarin decided his wife and daughter should travel first class, although most of the family traveled coach.

His daughter Katherine, traveling with a friend, recalled the trip well. "In those days, Russian first class was still a *bit behind* the rest of the world. The train looked like an old coal-fired, steel train from an American cowboy movie. Each compartment had two bunk beds and could be occupied by four people, regardless of sex. Each car had one bathroom, which was shared by approximately 32 travelers." As she recalled, "the bathroom floor was so worn that you could see the train tracks below through the spaces on the floor!"

As Katherine and her girlfriend learned, they would share their compartment with an unrelated man and a woman. The custom was for the man to step outside so the women could change in privacy at bedtime. After changing into her nightgown, Katherine realized the compartment was stifling hot. Since both she and her family had rented blankets, sheets, and pillows, Katherine opened the window to let in some fresh air. It was the man's turn to use the bathroom before retiring. Katherine noticed he was dressed only in a tee shirt and shorts. He closed the window on the way out. After he left, Katherine again opened the window. When the man returned, he saw the window open but said nothing, and just retired to the lower bunk across from Katherine. Since he had no pillow or pajamas, he cupped his hands behind his head, leaving his hairy armpits in full view.

"I turned over," said Katherine, recalling the incident almost three decades later. "But, it wasn't long before I realized the man reeked of body odor. I can still remember that disgusting, foul smell!"

Welcome Party

When the family arrived in Pskov the following morning, they were greeted personally by the smiling mayor and a contingent of ladies carrying bouquets of colorful flowers. "It was like going from being a piece of cargo to belle of the ball," smiled Katherine.

They were taken to City Hall, where they met all the local dignitaries and were awarded medals (a popular Russian tradition). They were given a tour of their tiny museum, where they saw Lenin's letter of instructions to his soldiers after Russia left World War I, dated 1919.

Meeting at Pskov City Hall

Lenin's instructions: "Do what you have to do to secure the area from departing German forces, but make every effort not to destroy the treasured Holmby Estate. It is our heritage." Apparently, the soldiers heeded the instructions, because Holmby was spared and turned into a hospital. But in recent years, with Soviet economic struggles, it had fallen into a state of disrepair.

Holmby Arrival

It was cool and cloudy by the time they arrived at the Gagarin family home site.

Seeing Holmby for the first time was a memorable moment for Gagarin. "It was one thing, seeing pictures and being told about the estate; it was quite another to stand in the vast fields where peasants toiled the land, and to walk through the large rooms with ornate moldings in such disrepair. For me, Holmby was a living metaphor for the class struggle I had read so much about."

Circa 1896. The Gagarin estate at Holmby in Russia

Years after that first family visit, Holmby was restored and turned into a state-run family vacation retreat. To this day, many working-class families travel great distances to spend parts of their summer at Holmby in Pskov.

Polaroid Camera

After the estate tour, the family was driven to the Gagarin family gravesite, which had been cleaned up for their visit. It was decorated with flowers and surrounded by a neat fence to separate it from the other poorly-kept gravesites. Katherine Gagarin described it as an "oasis in the middle of a mess."

Those in attendance began to pray in Russian, without any opening comments or the presence of a priest. Suddenly the thick clouds parted and a ray of sun fell directly on the grave marker. "It was like the hand of God touched Grandfather's site," said Ann.

Grandfather's unexpected sunshine

Two little boys from a nearby orphanage were playing in the graveyard. They stopped to watch Ann take a few pictures of the area with her Polaroid camera. The boys were amazed that the pictures developed right before their eyes. They had never seen such a thing. Ann waved to the boys, to see if they would like to have their picture taken. Since they didn't speak English, there was a bit of confusion until Gregory stepped in and explained.

Ann took a picture of the two boys with big smiles. She showed them how to rub the photo paper. Soon their images began to appear! They had never seen a picture of themselves.

Gregory spoke to them for a few minutes, and then they headed back to the orphanage. Ann asked her husband what they had said.

"They said the special lady made a miracle," said Gregory. "You know, like Christ on the mountain."

Ann laughed. "I would love to be a fly on the wall when they show the picture at the orphanage and try to explain what just happened."

Revisiting Max

When they returned to St. Petersburg, the family arranged for a comfortable suite at a local hotel where Ann, Gregory, and Katherine slept soundly. The next day, the family was going to meet his old friend Maxim Chibisov and *his* family at the Hall of Commanders.

The Hall was a grand affair. Center steps led up to a circular room lined with busts of notable commanders, like the Capitol Rotunda in Washington, D.C. "As I looked at (Chibisov's) bust for the first time," said Gagarin, "my mind was flooded with wonderful memories during a very difficult time."

Gagarin pays respects to his old friend

Gagarin noticed a few other things. The sculptor had perfectly captured Chibisov's sheepish smile. And his biography didn't mention Project Zebra by name; it merely referenced Max's involvement in a successful Russian-American Allied mission.

A few hours later, they visited the Chibisov family. The visit followed the usual Russian script: the elevator didn't work, and there were lots of hugs and kisses followed by massive amounts of food and drinks.

Circa 1991. Ann and Gregory Gagarin meet Yelena (upper right) and Emilia (center) for the first time.

To Ann, the good cheer and large variety of food were reminiscent of the train meal with the Gagarin family. After dinner, Yelena and her husband, Andrey, suggested a walk to digest their food and see a bit of New Russia. Gagarin noticed that the city seemed to function better, and the streets seemed neater and cleaner — but few people seemed to be smiling. Emilia read Gagarin's mind. "Things are better, but from what Father said, not yet like America."

When they returned to the apartment, Emilia opened a small room filled with the memorabilia their father had collected. Gagarin noticed the cigarette case. "Father said that case was very important to him," said Emilia.

They sat in the living room for hours. Gagarin mesmerized everybody (including Ann) with story after story about Project Zebra. The sisters asked questions and talked about detailed notations in their father's diary. They said they were working with the state to create a permanent exhibition of their father's legacy at a Homeland museum, preferably in Moscow. They had hired a journalist to turn their father's life — and his role in Project Zebra — into a book. Near midnight, the Gagarins were about to leave. Gregory turned and asked one last question. "Is there any way I can help?"

The sisters nodded. "Yes, we want to come to Elizabeth City. Father said he left a part of himself there."

Chapter 37

Stanley

Handsome and vital well into his 70s

Stanley Chernack retired from the service with the rank of Lieutenant Commander. He and his wife, Edith, and their two sons, Peter and Charles, moved to Los Altos, California, where they bought a home surrounded by apricot orchards.

In civilian life, Stanley worked for the Lockheed Corporation in nearby Mountain View, where he was an integral part of the management team that produced the Poseidon and Trident missiles for the Navy's nuclear submarines.

Gromyko's Invitation

Sometime in 1946, Chibisov and Tiertsiev's letters found their way to Andrei Gromyko, then the Russian Ambassador to the US and Minister of Soviet Foreign Affairs. He was pleased to invite Stanley to the Twenty-Seventh Anniversary Celebration of the Great October Revolution — Russia's most important holiday at the time. There, he was recognized for his wartime contributions to Soviet-American partnership. It would be the last such Russian event Stanley would attend.

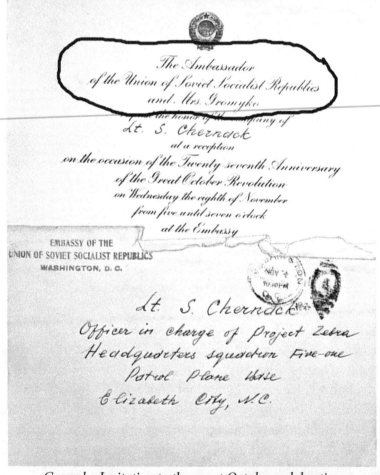

Gromyko Invitation to the great October celebration
at the Russian Embassy in Washington, D.C.

Gromyko became President of the Presidium of the Supreme Soviet in 1985, where he helped build the policy of Détente between the US and the USSR.[82] Gromyko never forgot the Zebra mission and he passed that fondness onto President Mikhail Gorbachev, who likewise passed it on to President Boris Yeltsin.

Yeltsin's Award

Boris Yeltsin became the first elected President of the New Russian Federation in June 1991. During his eight years in office (1991-1999), he attempted to improve both the Russian economy and its relations with the United States. Like most Russians, he wanted to continue to celebrate the victories and remember the heroes of the Great Patriotic War. In preparation for a May Day celebration, he learned of Chibisov, Project Zebra, and American Commander Stanley Chernack. He wished to offer Stanley a belated thank you from all Russians. On November 25, 1998, Yeltsin awarded Chernack a Russian Medal of Honor for his Project Zebra leadership.

Stanley's medal and date of issue

Chernack's son Peter urged him to go. For reasons we will never know, Chernack refused. The medal was issued on November 25, 1999, and sent to Stanley's home, where it has remained in storage until the writing of this book.

ПОСОЛ
РОССИЙСКОЙ ФЕДЕРАЦИИ
В США

AMBASSADOR
OF THE RUSSIAN FEDERATION
TO THE USA

Dear Sir,

On behalf of President Boris Yeltsin, the Russian Government and the entire Russian people, I am pleased to inform you that you have been awarded the Commemorative Medal "The 50th Anniversary of the Victory in the Great Patriotic War" (World War II).

This Medal is awarded to you in recognition of your courage and personal contribution to the Allied support of Russia during her fight for freedom against Nazi Germany.

Please accept my heartfelt congratulations and wishes for your good health, well-being and every success.

Sincerely,

Yuli M. VORONTSOV

Enclosures: Commemorative Medal, Medal Certificate.

Mum's the Word

According to his surviving family, Chernack rarely mentioned Project Zebra. He respected the fact that Zebra remained classified as top secret during his lifetime. Occasionally he would speak in general terms at conferences about Russian customs and traditions, but the Cold War and America's general anti-Russian sentiment precluded much else. While he gained the respect of numerous Russian officers and officials during the war, he never visited Russia or contacted any Russian or American Zebra teammates — other than Gagarin — after the war.

Belated Recognition

Lt. Gagarin's many Project Zebra contributions were also recognized by the Russian government. He was awarded a Russian Medal of Honor on the same day as Chernack. Unlike Chernack, however, the Lieutenant accepted his award at a formal state reception at the Russian Embassy in Washington, D.C.

Finally Declassified

For whatever reason, Project Zebra was not declassified until December 31, 2012. At the time of this writing in 2017, only one member of either side is still alive: my collaborator, the Russian Prince known as Lt. Gregory Gagarin, US Navy.

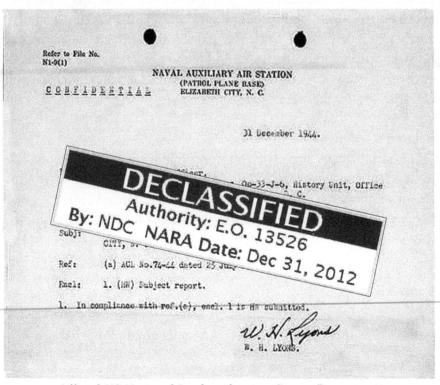

Official US National Declassification Center Document[83]

---

[83] National Declassification Center. The national archives contain the original Project launch only. There is no record of the final report. Until Now. Sealed among Stanley's papers is that final report dated November 12, 1945, and marked "Secret."

Chapter 38

One Extra Nomad

Gordon Sheet Metal and Roofing Company on S. Road Street

Charles Gordon was born and raised in Elizabeth City, and he served with distinction in the Pacific Theater during World War II. Like many returning veterans, he wondered what he was going to do next. Mechanically inclined by nature, he decided to take advantage of one of his veterans' benefits by going to technical school and then opening a commercial sheet metal business.

Before long, he was getting contacts for heating systems, roofs, and specialized assemblies for a wide variety of customers. In time, Gordon Sheet Metal Company provided for Gordon's family and more than 30 employees. Most remained with Charles for years, and one, Johnny Green, who grew up in the business, became Gordon's project manager around 1990. At 91, Charles still goes to the office every day, and, Johnny is still the company's project manager.

Little Ed Fearing

Sometime after the war ended, a giant amphibious Catalina appeared across from the Coast Guard base. It was similar in all respects to the Russian Nomad: dual machine gun turrets, large wings folded skyward, a cockpit filled with old dials and instruments, empty bomb bays, and a three-person sleeping area.

In 1965, Elizabeth City resident Ed Fearing was ten years old. He and his father and mother used to drive past the plane — now entirely covered in vines — on the way to visit Ed's cousin, Tommy Jones, who lived on the other side of the bay. One day on the way to his cousin's, Ed finally asked, "Dad, what's that plane doing there?"

"Some kind of PBY from the war. That's about all I know."

Ed was now even more curious. Reluctantly, Tommy agreed to ride over with Ed on their bikes to check it out. Ed wanted to explore inside. Tommy hesitated. "What about snakes?" Ed explained it was November and that *most* snakes only came out in the hot summer months.

"I remember I had to climb about 20 feet of vines to reach the cockpit at the top of the plane," said Ed. "Once inside, we were amazed. The dashboard was filled with instruments. Nothing had been removed. And a lot of the controls seemed to work. I could raise and lower the plane stick and manipulate the rudder controls. Even the pilot's seat was in good shape."

Over the next few weeks the boys returned frequently, usually around nightfall so that nobody could see them. With a flashlight in hand, they discovered machine gun turrets, giant storage bays, the navigator's station, and a fuselage that seemed to go on forever, with sleeping cots that hung from the ceiling.

Ed and his cousin in 1965. Ed today.

"Even the swivel seats in the two gun bays worked. There weren't any guns, but Tommy and I imagined firing in lots of different directions," recalled Ed. "But since it was my idea to explore the plane, we agreed I should be the pilot and co-pilot. Tommy agreed to be the gunner and navigator. We saw lots of action during our trips in the air. We battled the Germans, the Japanese, and anyone else we saw in the sky. I was a great pilot; we never got hit once by enemy fire."

Ed even recalled the time he imagined the radar not working, so he kicked it. There was a brief flash, then nothing. "It was kind of spooky," said Ed, "so I never did that again."

When the boys decided the war was over, they flew the plane to lots of new places. "We used to fly to the Bahamas, land the seaplane on the water, and then go swimming."

Ed also described the time they, as children with vivid imaginations, saw a shark in the clear waters and had to outrace it to get back to the safety of the plane. In time, the boys grew up and graduated to more adult activities.

During the next 50 years, the plane just sat in the field. Vines and weeds completely covered the now-rusted plane. One day, Ed was driving his pickup truck down Consolidated Avenue on the way to work when he noticed that the vines had been cleared away and the plane was gone.

Phone Call

One day, during the year 2000, sheet metal owner Charles Gordon received a call from a man who identified himself as a World War II memorabilia collector living in Northern California. The man asked if Charles would be interested in disassembling the WWII Nomad, which sat across from the Coast Guard base on Consolidated Boulevard, and transporting it to California.

Charles explained that he could do it, but "the costs might be prohibitive." The man explained he was a successful businessman who could afford it. The still skeptical Charles said that for this kind of job, he would require 50 percent of the estimated costs in advance.

Again, the man responded without hesitation: "No problem." He also said he and his son would handle all the transportation arrangements.

To create a proper estimate, Charles visited the site to figure how much time and effort it would take to remove the years of plant growth, then disassemble and load the plane on trucks. In addition, the plane would have to be purchased from the Coast Guard.

To his surprise, Charles learned when he spoke to the commander that the Coast Guard had dragged the plane off the base after Project Zebra ended because the large plane sat in one of only two repair hangers that the Coast Guard owned, and they needed the space for active search-and-find missions.

Charles explained about the project for the Californian and asked how much the Coast Guard wanted for the plane. "How much do I want?" laughed the commander. "Just getting the thing out of here is payment enough. I've never been able to get anyone in the Navy interested in taking back the plane. It's almost like the factory in Philadelphia accidentally produced one extra plane for the Russians."

Charles called the California man back with an estimate, which was approved. He said," The money [will] be on the way tomorrow." Two days later, a young man showed up with a bag of money and three long haul trucks. He explains he was the buyer's son and would help supervise the plane's disassembly, as well as its placement and securing on the trucks.

Charles called his supervisor, John, to explain the project. At first, John thought it was a joke. Clearing the brush away and disassembling the large and small sections of the plane — without damaging anything — took about five days. The man paid Charles in full, with cash, and left with the trucks. He didn't even ask for a receipt. Charles lost the buyer's contact information and didn't think about the matter for another 16 years. At that point, a writer — me — showed up at his door, asking him about his recollections of Project Zebra. At first, Charles said, "I was away during those years. Don't know anything." Then, he paused and told the story you have just read. I told him the whole thing sounded incredulous. He, in turn, picked up the phone and called his field manager, John.

Charles does a story check with John

"John... Charles here. Got a few minutes? There's this man here who wants to know about that old plane we got rid of back when."

John then got on the phone and repeated Charles' story, almost verbatim. He also had one other observation: "The son was good looking. Dark wavy hair, like one of those movie stars."

Chapter 39

Max Revisits Elizabeth City

Gagarin entrance at Chevy Chase, MD, home built to recall Holmby in Pskov

Three years later, the Chibisov sisters. Yelena and Emilia, arrived at Dulles Airport in Washington, D.C., where they were greeted by the Gagarin family with three kisses each and firm hugs. Yelena was pleased. "You haven't forgotten the Russian way." The plan was to rest and talk for a few days at the Gagarin home, then drive to Elizabeth City, some 200 miles south.

As they pulled up to a gate with a long driveway, the sisters noticed the sign: "Gagarin at Holmby."

The sign immediately brought back memories of newspaper stories about the original Gagarin estate at Holmby in Pskov, Russia, before the revolution. This home, while different from the original estate, had many striking similarities. "I couldn't recreate Grandfather's place exactly," smiled Gagarin, "But the American Prince did the best he could."

The sisters could not believe Gagarin's pride in his Russian heritage: his great-great-grandfather, the noted artist Prince Grigory Gagarin; and Imperial Russia.

Father's Wings

After a distinctly American meal of steak on the barbecue with all the fixings, a few toasts, and more hugs, Gagarin took the sisters on a tour of his home. It ended in the spacious dining room, where every inch of the main table was filled with Project Zebra pictures. Emilia picked up a picture of her father fishing in the Atlantic Ocean. "Never saw. Father loved to fish. I think he was always a little disappointed he didn't have a son to tag along."

Yelena noticed a glass cabinet stocked with memorabilia. Gagarin explained the significance of some of his favorite pieces: the dented metal icon that saved his father's life as he fled the Bolsheviks, and an oversized silver certificate. "These bills don't even look like real money," said Emilia.

Trust me," smiled Gagarin, "Those big bills are worth big money: two hundred dollars each, maybe more."

"Did my father know that?"

"Not exactly," responded Gagarin, knowing certain things were better left unspoken.

Yelena noticed Red Army wings resting on a piece of dark blue leather. "These look exactly like my father's."

Gagarin memorabilia case with Max's wings

"These *belonged to* your father. He gave them to me just before he boarded his final flight back to Russia."

The sisters had tears in their eyes as they rubbed the piece. The significance of Max's gesture was understood.

Elizabeth City

As Gagarin drove into town, the sisters noticed the sign: *Elizabeth City, Harbor of Hospitality.*

Mayor Peel at the Harbor of Hospitality

Gagarin drove the sisters around the main shopping area; he realized many of the places he had frequented during the days of Project Zebra were gone or had been renovated. They stopped in front of a building that was now an arts center. "This used to be Chesson's Department Store. Before every Soviet left for home, they would load up with American products," recalled Gagarin.

"Father never mentioned that," said Emilia.

"I think that was one of those little Elizabeth City secrets. I heard stories from the men that Max charmed the clerks into selling his men more than the standard rationing allotments. He'd explain the difficulties in the Soviet Union, and make people feel sorry."

Emilia was puzzled. "How could he explain Soviet difficulties? He barely spoke English."

"From the amount of stuff that came back to the base in the Colonel's car and the taxi cabs, I would say they managed somehow. All I know is when I went to town for a haircut or a meal, I was always asked the same question: 'Lieutenant, when are the boys planning to leave?' They wanted to make sure the shelves were filled to the brim for the departing crews. By the time they left, the shelves looked like a state-run store in Moscow."

While the sisters enjoyed hearing about how Max and the boys shopped and played, their primary interest was in visiting the Elizabeth City Naval Base.

As they toured the base, Gagarin explained that the property was a dual facility used by both the Navy and the Coast Guard. The sisters understood the role of the Navy but wondered about the mission of the Coast Guard, a term which was unfamiliar in the USSR during the war. Gagarin explained that German U-boats had been spotted within 20 miles of the Outer Banks of North Carolina. The women were surprised, to say the least.

*Chibisov's daughters, Gagarin, and the Elizabeth City
Coast Guard base commanders*

Gagarin pointed to an empty lot. "That's where your father and I and the other officers lived. We ate the same food, played the same games in the lounge, and slept in the same barracks."

He took them to the gymnasium and explained movie night. "So, this is where Father meet Betty Grable and Lana Turner," smiled Yelena. "He mentioned them many times. You know, in those days, Soviet movies were not like American movies."

Gagarin chuckled. "I do remember that. Your father just loved American musicals. The sexier, the better!"

As the three continued their self-guided tour, Gagarin fondly recalled Zebra World Headquarters. "We shared a lot of coffee and a lot of laughs in that old hut."

Two Naval air officers approached. "Can we help you folks?" Gagarin explained who he was. "We heard bits about that mission," said one of the officers. "But we thought everyone was gone."

Gagarin smiled, "I guess I'm the last man standing."

They shook Gagarin's hand, "Sir, thank you for your service."

The two officers realized they had not said anything to the sisters. "Are you all related?"

Yelina, in a heavy Russian accent, explained who they were. The officers' mouths opened. "Nobody will ever believe this. Let's get a few pictures?"

Soon, a base photographer was taking pictures of the five by the bank of the Pasquotank River. One of the officers stared at the river. "Hard to believe they never found that plane or the bodies."

As Gagarin and the sisters started to leave, one of the officers pointed to an enormous modern structure down the road. The officer explained that it was the site of the original repair facility for the Naval blimps and the Soviet Nomads. "That old wooden building burned down sometime after the war. Took a lot of history with it."

Gagarin made one last stop: the new Albemarle Museum. From past discussions with local area reporters, he knew the museum had some background and interest in Project Zebra. There, Gagarin and the sisters met two of the curators, Leonard Lanier and Clay Swindell. Gagarin had brought along some pictures and the girls talked about their father's fond memories. They all agreed that someday, somehow, a Project Zebra exhibition would be a fitting remembrance of an important moment lost in time.

The Gift

For Yelena and Emilia, the time spent with the Gagarins at Holmby in Chevy Chase, Maryland, was more than just a memorable experience. They learned about the unique place held in Russian history by the Gagarin family. As Emilia said, "We learned why the American with Russian blood was so important and so respected."

Е.М. РУБИНА, Э.М. ТЕЛЯТНИКОВА

ЧЕРЕЗ МАТЕРИКИ
И ОКЕАНЫ

Maxim's life of accomplishment in book form

The sisters explained they had fulfilled one of the objectives they spoke about in Russia. A book about their father's life, entitled *Across Three Oceans; Two Continents,* had been completed in collaboration with two reporters, E.M. Telyatikova and E.M. Ruina. Emilia proudly gave Ann and Gregory an autographed copy in Russian. "Maybe someday," said Yelena, "the story of the Zebra mission will be told in America."

The two sisters explained they had donated virtually all of their father's memorabilia to a permanent Maxim Chibisov exhibition now located at the Allied Lend-Lease Museum in Moscow. "You must visit on your next trip home," said Emilia.

Gagarin also took the sisters to the Russian Embassy, where the door was always open to him. They met with some officials who praised their father's career accomplishments, although they freely admitted they knew nothing of Project Zebra.

Eventually, the Gagarins drove the sisters back to Dulles Airport. The four hugged one final time. "We are so glad you have shown us where Father worked in the wilds of the United States," Emilia said.

Home at Last

In May 2017, the Honorable Joseph Peel, Mayor of Elizabeth City, received a call from the Russian Embassy in Washington, D.C. The man introduced himself as Maxim Alekseyev, Chief of the Russian side office of US-Russia Joint Commission on POW/MIAs (USRJC).[84] He wished to discuss Project Zebra.

Peel assumed it was part of the continued search for the Soviet personnel that perished after takeoff in the Pasquotank River, some 70 years ago.

"It is about another matter," Alekseyev said.

Maxim and his American joint commission partner, James Connel Jr., arrived a few weeks later with a folio in hand. During the meeting, city officials learned that the American and Russian governments wanted to belatedly honor this long-forgotten page in history.

---

[84] USRJC was established in 1992 by George H. W. Bush and Boris Yeltsin. See References.

(l to r) Dr. James Connel and Maxim Alekseyev

Alekseyev pulled out a drawing of a grand monument, some 12-15 feet high, with a British, an American, and a Soviet soldier standing in front of a replica of the giant Nomad.

Project Zebra bronze memorial to be erected in Elizabeth City

While Project Zebra was primarily an American-Russian initiative, it would not have been successful with the mission's silent partner, the British Royal Air Force. The British didn't finance, produce, or train Zebra crews, but they did play an integral intermediary role because of their prior experience flying a modified version of the giant amphibious Catalina, and because of their strategically located air bases.

"It would be like the Moskovskiy Prospect monument," said Alekseyev.

The Council was told the monument would take a year to be funded, produced, shipped, and installed by the Russian Government.

Allied Monument at the entrance to Moscow

Not a word was spoken about the political difficulties of the moment, but Mayor Peel took the project to be an olive branch on the part of the Russians. Other council members were dubious, given the current state of Russian-American relations. After some debate, the project was unanimously approved on the evening of May 22, 2017. The monument is expected to be installed in summer or fall of 2018, with an accompanying exhibit at Albemarle Museum.

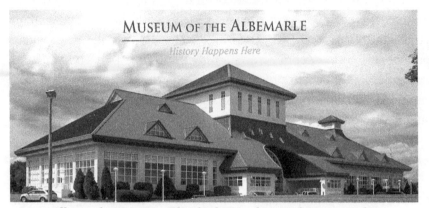

Albemarle Museum, Elizabeth City, home of American history

The face of the Soviet soldier is expected to be Major General Maxim Chibisov. So, in a way never imagined, Maxim's personal dream to revisit Elizabeth City may ultimately be realized.

Thank You, America

Don't know where, don't know when, but we'll meet again some sunny day,

Thank You, Russia.

Don't know where, don't know when, but we'll meet again some sunny day,

Afterword

Young Lieutenant Gagarin reminisces at his home 73 years later

Dear Reader,

I hope you have enjoyed *Project Zebra*. My name is Gregory Gagarin, and as of June 2017, I am the last living survivor of this amazing cross-cultural adventure. I'm now 95 and, unfortunately, completely blind.

I have long wanted to codify the story for my family and my legacy, but somehow life got in the way. Magically, as it sometimes happens, Matt Crisci appeared. He has taken an extraordinary amount of time out of his life to reconstruct all the pieces. I have helped with my documents, memories, and pictures… but he has told the entire story, some of which surprised even me.

My only regret is when you read this letter, you will realize because of my blindness, I will never be able to see the final book. But I have absolutely no regrets: I've lived a full life, have a great family, a ton of friends, and more memories than any person could ever imagine.

As twilight approaches, I have one last dream. Perhaps the publication of this book in some small way will shed light on how two great nations — my parents' Russian Homeland and my American Homeland — can work together to make this a better world for all.

With the greatest respect,

Gregory Gagarin

MAYOR
JOSEPH W. PEEL
MAYOR PRO-TEM
ANITA HUMMER
CITY MANAGER
RICHARD C. OLSON
CITY CLERK
VIVIAN WHITE, NCCMC

CITY COUNCIL MEMBERS
JEAN M. BAKER
MICHAEL E. BROOKS
RAYMOND T. DONNELLY
DARIUS J. HORTON
RICKEY E. KING
TONY STIMATZ
JOHNNIE B. WALTON

CITY OF ELIZABETH CITY

June 12, 2017

Dear Readers:

It is indeed a pleasure for me to congratulate my friend, Matt Crisci, on the completion of this remarkable book, which, for the first time, eloquently tells the true story of Project Zebra.

This little-known, top-secret project bore huge historical significance; and his book details Elizabeth City, North Carolina's contribution to the successful outcome of this project and hence of World War II.

I have often heard stories about the Naval Air Station and its airships located in Elizabeth City during World War II. But until learning of the entire scope of Project Zebra story, I was not aware that our small town played such an important part in this top-secret project to train Soviet airmen to fly the planes that we Americans had built for them to seek and destroy German U-boats and Japanese submarines in the Atlantic and Pacific theaters.

I am encouraged by this show of brotherhood and the willingness of our countries to work together at that time to defeat a very real evil. This story certainly highlights the importance and power of international partnerships and alliances between and among countries during war time. A lesson we don't need to forget today.

Mathew, thank you for telling this inspiring story for our future generations.

Sincerely,

Dr. Joseph W. Peel
Mayor

POST OFFICE BOX 347 • ELIZABETH CITY, NORTH CAROLINA 27907-0347 • (252) 338-3981

References

Books

Alia, Valerie. *Names & Nunavut: Culture and Identity in the Inuit Homeland*. New York: Berghahn Books, 2007.

Berry, Marjorie Ann. *Legendary Locals of Elizabeth City*. Charleston: Arcadia Publishing, 2014.

Birstein, Vadim. *SMERSH: Stalin's Secret Weapon*. London: Biteback Publishing, 2013.

Butler, Susan, ed. *My Dear Mr. Stalin: The Complete Correspondence of Franklin D. Roosevelt and Joseph V. Stalin*. New Haven: Yale University Press, 2006.

Butler, Susan. *Roosevelt and Stalin: Portrait of a Partnership*. New York: Knopf Doubleday, 2016.

Crisci, M.G. *7 Days in Russia*. Carlsbad: Orca Publishing USA, 2014.

Crisci, M.G. *Call Sign, White Lily*. Carlsbad: Orca Publishing USA, 2012.

Dolitsky, Alexander B. *Allies in Wartime: The Alaska-Siberia Airway During World War II*. Juneau: Alaska-Siberia Research Center, 2007.

E.M. Ruina, E.M., and Telyatiikova, E.M. *Across the Continent and the Ocean*. R&C Dynamics, 2011.

Fitzpatrick, Sheila. *Everyday Stalinism: Ordinary Life in Extraordinary Times: Soviet Russia in the 1930s*. Oxford: Oxford University Press, 1999.

Freeze, Gregory L. *Russia: A History*. Oxford: Oxford University Press, 2009.

Gagarin, Elizabeth. "Ah Fu's Escape," in unpublished diary, 1975.

Hilberg, Raul. *The Destruction of the European Jews*. New Viewpoints Press, 1973.

Hoffman, David L. Stalinist Values: *Cultural Norms of Soviet Modernity, 1917-1941*. Ithaca: Cornell University Press, 2003.

Hosking, Geoffrey. *History of the USSR, 1917-1992*. Fontana Press, 1993.

Kagarlitsky, Boris. *Russia under Yeltsin and Putin: Neo-Liberal Autocracy*. Pluto Press, 2002.

Katsenelinboigen, Aron. "Colored Markets in the Soviet Union." *Soviet Studies* XXIX, no. 1 (1977): 62-85.

Kumanev, G. *The People's Commissars of Stalin Speak*. Smolensk Rusich, 2005.

Leonov, Viktor. *Blood on the Shores: Soviet SEALs in World War II.* New York: Random House, 1994.

Martynowych, Orest T. *The Showman and the Ukrainian Cause: Folk Dance, Film, and the Life of Vasile Avramenko.* Winnipeg: University of Manitoba Press, 2014.

Odom, William. *The Soviet Volunteers: Modernization and Bureaucracy in Public Mass Organization.* Princeton: Princeton University Press, 1973.

Pinkowski, Edward. "Soviet Trainees in U.S.A. in World War II." *The Russian Review* 6, no. 1 (1946): 11-16.

Articles

"U.S. Department of the Navy: Project Zebra Declassified, E.0. 13526," last modified December 2012, https://www.fold3.com/image/302060700

"Soviet Casualty Estimates," Wikipedia, https://en.wikipedia.org/wiki/World_War_II_casualties_of_the_Soviet_Union

Carroll, George. *U.S. Secretly Trained Red Navy Pilots.* New York Journal-American, 1946. Print.

United Press Int'l. *Soviets Received 100 Seaplanes.* New York Times, 1946. Print.

"Crashed Nomad Discovered in Norway, 2007," K.T. Sorens, http://ktsorens.tihlde.org/flyvrak/andotten.html

"Lend-Lease Airforce," http://lend-lease.airforce.ru/english/articles/commandeur/

"History of Catalina," http://www.catalina.org.uk/catalina-history/

"History of the Consolidated Aircraft Company," Wikipedia, https://en.wikipedia.org/wiki/Consolidated_PBY_Catalina#Other_Users

"Nomads in America," http://www.polarpost.ru/forum/viewtopic.php?f=55&t=2041#p16115

"History of the Naval Aircraft Factory, Wikipedia, https://en.wikipedia.org/wiki/Naval_Aircraft_Factory

"History of the Flying Boat," Wikipedia, https://en.wikipedia.org/wiki/Flying_boat

"Airplane Specifications," https://www.google.com/#q=737+height

"Airplane Specifications," http://pbycatalina.com/specifications/

"American Aviation History," The Aviation History Online Museum, http://www.aviation-history.com/douglas/dc3.html

"Secret Mission Uncovered, 2013," The Virginian Pilot, last modified July 16, 2014, http://pilotonline.com/news/details-come-to-light-about-wwii-secret-mission-in-n/article_ef7c0168-20c6-5e9b-bc60-303c11895f9f.html

"Odessa Resident Missing," The Times-News, last modified September 14, 2015, http://www.thetimesnews.com/article/20150914/news/150919440://www.odessitclub.org/archive/stories_

"Military History from Another Perspective," https://www.military-history.org/articles/war-culture-military-drinking.htm

"World War II changed how America drank: Live from Tales of the Cocktail," The Times-Picayune, last modified July 16, 2015, http://www.nola.com/drink/index.ssf/2015/07/world_war_ii_changed_how_ameri.html

Hitler, Adolph. *Führer's Directive 21. December 18, 1940.*
Retrieved from
United States Department of State, Documents on German Foreign Policy: Archives of the German Foreign Ministry.

"Difference Between Communism and Nazism," http://www.differencebetween.net/miscellaneous/difference-between-communism-and-nazism/#ixzz4Yt65Faw9

"Communism versus Nazism.," http://www.differencebetween.net/miscellaneous/difference-between-communism-and-nazism/

"U.S.-Soviet Alliance, 1941-1945," US Department of State, https://history.state.gov/milestones/1937-1945/us-soviet

"Stalin as Puppet Master," http://www.historynet.com/stalin-the-puppetmaster.htm

"Stalin's Purges," http://russiapedia.rt.com/of-russian-origin/stalins-purges/

"Translating Russian," http://www.russianlessons.net/lessons/lesson1_alphabet.php

"Seventeen Moments in Soviet History," http://soviethistory.macalester.edu/index.php

"NKVD and Soviet Counter-Intelligence," Wikipedia, http://en.wikipedia.org/wiki/NKVD

"The Neutrality Acts, 1930s," US Department of State, https://history.state.gov/milestones/1921-1936/neutrality-acts

"History of SMERSH," Wikipedia, https://en.wikipedia.org/wiki/SMERSH

"Stanley Chernack, the Man," Los Altos Town Crier, last modified August 21, 2007, https://www.losaltosonline.com/news/sections/news/220-latc-sections/comment/comment-archive/16743-J15067

"Blue Angel Nightclub," http://www.elearnportal.com/resources/military/blue-angels-history

"Quonset Hut Fundamentals," http://www.polarinertia.com/may04/quonset01.htm

"Some Choice Bits of Slang From American Soldiers Serving in WWII," Slate, last modified November 11, 2013, http://www.slate.com/blogs/the_vault/2013/11/11/military_slang_terms_used_by_soldiers_in_wwii.html

"Food and Clothing in the Soviet Union," Wikipedia, https://en.wikipedia.org/wiki/Consumer_goods_in_the_Soviet_Union

"Soviet Rationing," http://histclo.com/essay/war/ww2/cou/sov/home/shf-food.html

"Consumer Goods in the Soviet Union," Wikipedia, https://en.wikipedia.org/wiki/Consumer_goods_in_the_Soviet_Union

"Everyday Hardship: The Red Army Soldier's Diet," Keep Calm and Remember, last modified January 8, 2015, https://keepcalmandremember.wordpress.com/2015/01/08/everyday-hardship-the-red-army-soldiers-diet/

"Jokes as the Truth about Soviet Socialism," Christie Davies, https://www.folklore.ee/folklore/vol46/davies.pdf

"Soviet Poster Collection," Wright Museum of Art, http://www.reeec.illinois.edu/teachers/lesson/documents/soviet_posters.pdf

"CHAPAYEV – Film (Movie) Plot and Review," Film Reference, http://www.filmreference.com/Films-Ca-Chr/Chapayev.html

"The Cinema of Stalinism," Film Reference, http://www.filmreference.com/encyclopedia/Romantic-Comedy-Yugoslavia/Russia-and-Soviet-Union-The-cinema-of-Stalinism-1930-1941.html

"Tourism Impacts on Dare County," Carolina Population Center, last modified July 14, 2015, http://demography.cpc.unc.edu/2015/07/14/tourism-impacts-on-dare-county/

"Prominent Russians: Lyubov Orlova," Russiapedia, http://russiapedia.rt.com/prominent-russians/cinema-and-theater/lyubov-orlova/

"1930's Hollywood Musicals Lift Our Spirits," Hollywood Movie Memories, http://www.hollywoodmoviememories.com/articles/musicals-articles/1930s-hollywood-musicals-lift.php

"Russian Women," Master Russian, http://masterrussian.com/russianculture/russian_women.htm

"The Historic Role that Soviet Women Played in Defeating the Nazis in World War II," Global Research, last modified March 8, 2014, https://www.globalresearch.ca/how-the-west-ignores-women-as-actors-in-otherized-societies-a-sociological-unraveling-of-the-logos-of-the-soviet-amazons/5372529

"The Blue Angels," Sun-Sentinel, http://articles.sun-sentinel.com/1998-05-01/specialsection/9805050175_1_navy-blue-angels-demonstration-pilots-plane-pilots

"Mildred Bailey, Blue Angel Years," http://nyapril1946.blogspot.com/2010/07/mildred-bailey-at-blue-angel.html Blue Angel Nightclub

"Russian Zebra Soldier," Olga Ivanova, http://izvestia.ru/news/302380#ixzsomM7

"Bobby Short: Icon of Manhattan Song and Style, Dies at 80," The New York Times, last modified March 21, 2005, http://www.nytimes.com/2005/03/21/arts/music/21cnd-short.html?_r=0

"History of Virginia Dare Hotel," Emporis, https://www.emporis.com/buildings/223640/virginia-dare-hotel-elizabeth-city-nc-usa

"Black Market,"Encyclopedia.com, http://www.encyclopedia.com/social-sciences-and-law/law/crime-and-law-enforcement/black-market

"Bolshevik Visions," PBS, http://www.pbs.org/wgbh/commandingheights/lo/countries/ru/ru_economic.html

"Russia's shadow economy down to 35% of GDP in 2011," RT News, last modified February 14, 2013, https://www.rt.com/business/russia-shadow-economy-gdp-203/

"Putin voices grievances as huge parade marks 70th anniversary of victory," The Guardian, last modified May 9, 2015, https://www.theguardian.com/world/2015/may/09/russia-marks-victory-day-red-square-parade-putin

"Putin Rolls Out Nukes For Holiday Celebrating Victory Over Nazis," The Daily Beast, last modified May 10, 2015, http://www.thedailybeast.com/articles/2015/05/10/putin-rolls-out-nukes-for-holiday-celebrating-victory-over-nazis.html

"Grier School for Girls," https://www.grier.org/page

"Not-So-Secret Weapon: The Norden Bombsight," History Net, last modified March 9, 2017, http://www.historynet.com/not-so-secret-weapon-the-norden-bombsight.htm

"Ecole Champlain, the French summer camp," https://ecolechamplain.wordpress.com/

"Russian Spetsnaz," Systema Spetsnaz, http://www.systemaspetsnaz.com/russian-spetsnaz-gru-kgb-fsb-mvd

"The Soviet PBY Catalinas of World War II," VVS Air War, last modified March 7, 2017, https://vvsairwar.com/2017/03/07/the-soviet-pby-catalinas-of-wwii/

"Kodiak: The Emerald Isle," Travel Alaska, https://www.travelalaska.com/destinations/communities/kodiak.aspx

"History of the Sakhalin Islands," Wikipedia, https://en.wikipedia.org/wiki/Sakhalin

"Gotthard tunnel: World's longest and deepest rail tunnel opens in Switzerland," BBC, last modified June 1, 2016,http://www.bbc.com/news/world-europe-36423250

"Maakhir State of Somalia," https://maakhir.wordpress.com/2007/08/23/maakhir-state-of-somalia-faces-challenges-and-obstacles/

"Freshwater Fishing," The Yakutat Lodge, http://yakutatlodge.com/freshwater-fishing/

"Life in Yakutat," http://www.yakutatalaska.com/maps.html

"Purchase of Alaska, 1867," US Department of State, https://history.state.gov/milestones/ 1866-1898/alaska-purchase

"Kharlovka River: Salmon Asset," http://www.kharlovka.com/kharlovka-salmon-river/

"Lake Baikal: World's Largest, Deepest Lake," LiveScience, last modified January 26, 2017, http://www.livescience.com/57653-lake-baikal-facts.html

"A Comparison of the US and Soviet Economies: Evaluating the Performance of the Soviet System," US Central Intelligence Agency, https://www.cia.gov/library/readingroom/docs/ DOC_0000497165.pdf

Glaze, Helene M. "Lenin's New Economic Policy: What it was and how it Changed the Soviet Union," Inquiries Journal, http://www.inquiriesjournal.com/articles/59/2/lenins-new-economic-policy-what-it-was-and-how-it-changed-the-soviet-union

"Life in the USSR Under Stalin," C.N. Trueeman, historylearningsite.co.uk.

"Truman Records Impressions of Stalin," The /history Channel, http://www.history.com/ this-day-in-history/truman-records-impressions-of-stalin

"The bliss of flying," Sputnik News Agency and Radio, February 21, 2008, https:// sputniknews.com/voiceofrussia/radio_broadcast/2248834/2316426/

"Maxim Chibisov Exhibition," http://englishrussia.com/2012/05/09/unique-lend-lease-museum-in-moscow/

"The Allies and Lend-Lease Museum" Sputnik News Agency and Radio, November 2, 2007, https://sputniknews.com/voiceofrussia/2007/11/02/160300.html

"Who was responsible for the USSR Collapse?" http://debate.org/debates/783-gorbachev-was-responsible-for-the-collapse-of-the-ussr/#yes1

"The St. Petersburg Polytechnic Institute," http://www.spbstu.ru/university/about-the-university/history/laboratories-classrooms/

"The 'salo cult' in Ukraine: more than just a food," Krones, February 10, 2013, https:// blog.krones.com/blog/people/the-salo-cult-in-the-ukraine-more-than-just-a-food/?lang=en

"U.S.-Russia Joint Commission on POW/MIAs," Wikipedia, https://en.wikipedia.org/wiki/ U.S.%E2%80%93Russia_Joint_Commission_on_POW/MIAs

"Project Zebra Final Mission Reports," from Historical Archives of Stanley Chernack

"M. Chibisov and B. Tiertsiev letters to U.S. Naval Command.," from Historical Archives of Stanley Chernack.

"Gromyko Made Soviet President by Gorbachev," The New York Times, July 2, 1985, http:// www.nytimes.com/1985/07/03/world/gromyko-made-soviet-president-by-gorbachev.html

"Boris Yeltsin, President of Russia," Encyclopedia Britannica, https://www.britannica.com/ biography/Boris-Yeltsin

310

"FDR and the Election of 1944," Matthew Dalek, https://gilderlehrman.org/history-by-era/
world-war-ii/essays/franklin-delano-roosevelt%E2%80%94four-term-
president%E2%80%94and-election-1944

"Novoye Russkoye Slovo Newspaper," http://www.inforeklama.com/partners/newspapers/
nrs/info.htm

"Boris Novyy Reports of Performance. 2001," translated from Russian by Dr. James G.
Connell, U.S. Defense POW/MIA Accounting Agency, 2005.

Interviews and Conversations

Vladimir Alenikov (Russian writer/producer/director; Moscow, RU).

Maxim Andreevich (Russian Director, POW Institute; Russian Embassy, Washington, D.C.).

Cindy Beamon (Reporter, *Daily Advance Newspaper*; Elizabeth City, NC).

Rebecca Chernack (daughter-in-law, Stanley Chernack).

Emilia Chibisov (daughter of Maxim Chibisov; Moscow, RU).

James G. Connell, PhD (director of POW Institute, U.S. Defense POW/MIA Accounting
Agency; Washington D.C.).

George Converse (military historian; Elizabeth City, NC) .

Elizabeth City Library (Elizabeth City, NC).

Edward Fearing (resident and child Nomad pilot; Elizabeth City, NC).

Gregory Gagarin (notes, records, logbooks; Chevy Chase, MD).

Allen Gallop (resident; Elizabeth City, NC).

Charles Gordon (business owner; Elizabeth City, NC).

Leonard Lanier (Assistant Collections Specialist, Museum of the Albemarle; Elizabeth City.
NC).

Joseph Peel (Mayor; Elizabeth City, NC).

Alexander Potemkin (Executive Director, American-Russian Cultural Cooperation Center;
Washington, D.C.).

Flora Robinson (104-year-old resident; Elizabeth City, NC).

Valentin Sapunov, PhD. (professor, St. Petersburg State University; St. Petersburg, RU).

Edwin Swindell (Director of Collections, Museum of the Albemarle; Elizabeth City, NC).

Frank Weeks (resident, child nomad navigator; Elizabeth City, NC).

Yury Zaitsev (Director, Russian Cultural Center; Washington, D.C.).

Oleg Zhiganov (First Secretary, Russian Embassy; Washington, D.C.).

Peter Zwack (retired U.S. General, Minister Defense; Moscow, RU)

Photography, Document, and Illustration Credits

American-Russian Cultural Cooperation Foundation.

Archives of the Elizabeth City Historical Association, Elizabeth City, NC

Archives of George Converse, Elizabeth City Historian.

Archives of the Gregory Gagarin Family, Chevy Chase, MD.

Archives of Maxim Chibisov Family, Moscow, RU.

Archives of Stanley Chernack, Burbank, CA.

Library of Congress, Washington, D.C.

Lilia Litvyak Museum, Krasny Luch, Eastern Ukraine.

London Evening Standard, 1939.

Offices of Mayor Joseph Peel, Elizabeth City, NC.

Rob Row, Cartoonist. Retrieved from
https://www.emaze.com/@AQZOQCCT/the-cold-war-

Russian and Slavic Resources. Retrieved from
http: //archives.dickinson.edu/russian_resources

Southern Zebra Route Map. Retrieved from
http://nostomaniac.ca/thb-ww2/maps/Map-1945-feb-01.html#prettyPhoto

Life Under Communism. Illustrations.
The University of Iowa. Retrieved from
Digital.llb.uiowa.edu/tc

U.S. Navy Historical Archives. Washington, D.C.

THE WORLD OF

M.G. Crisci

Stories that entertain. People you'll remember.
Literature that matters.

Twitter.com/worldofmgcrisci
YouTube.com/worldofmgcrisci
f Facebook.com/worldofmgcrisci

Buy now at
amazon.com >

TRAVEL PHOTOJOURNAL

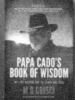

HUMOR AND WISDOM

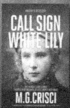

WOMAN'S ACCOMPLISHMENT

POLITICAL SATIRE

SUCCESS AND EXCESS

BIG APPLE SHORT STORIES

INSPIRATION AND WIT

WW2 HISTORY

PERIOD ROMANCE

SEXUAL HARRASSMENT

INSIDE WALL STREET

WHITE COLLAR CRIME

Learn more at www.mgcrisci.com

CPSIA information can be obtained
at www.ICGtesting.com
Printed in the USA
LVHW051232030320
648825LV00003BA/132